GOD'S PUNISHMENT

JULIÁN DE LA CHICA

GOD'S PUNISHMENT

IRREVERENCE
GROUP MUSIC

God's Punishment is a work of fiction. Space and time have been rearranged to suit the convenience of the book, and with the exception of public figures, any resemblance to persons living or dead is coincidental. The opinions expressed are those of the characters and should not be confused with the author's. The author in no way represents the companies, corporations, or brands mentioned in this book. The likeness of historical/famous figures have been used fictitiously; the author does not speak for or represent these people. All opinions expressed in this book are the author's, or fictional.

Printed in the United Stated of America
First Edition

Designed by Irreverence Group Music
ISBN 978-0-578-99377-5

Irreverence Group Music | Brooklyn, NY

It was considered incurable, mutilating, and shameful.

In 1905, the government of Colombia decreed the systematic exclusion of “lepers” and ordered them to be confined in leprosariums.

Some called it leprosy. Others called it *God’s Punishment.*

To all the victims of Agua de Dios.

Based on True Events

1
Isabel & Tomás

Whenever I talk or think about Isabel, I end up spoiling my day and getting into a bad mood. It's strange what I feel—like an unbridled mixture of things, of forgetfulness and confused memories. And I say it's strange, because I shouldn't feel anything, at least not now, after so long. When I think of her, sometimes I think of how happy I could have been, and that terrifies me. Other times I think of her with a certain hatred, which also terrifies me—but the truth is that the memories I have, I don't even know if they are memories or the inventions of my memory anymore. I must be careful, I think, with what I remember and what I say.

I met Isabel when I first arrived in Bogotá, at her home, during one of those famous and lavish soirees that her parents used to offer. I attended by chance, not because I was invited. Pedro Valenzuela and his wife Cristina (I was staying with them) invited me that night. They were determined to take me to every party there was and to introduce me to all their friends and relatives. It was night after night the same routine: endless dinners, dances and concerts, all surrounded by banal and hypocritical people.

Isabel belonged to an aristocratic, wealthy, and prominent family. They were famous for their philanthropy (especially of the arts) and their political work, where they had quite a lot of influence, by the way. But perhaps what Isabel's parents were most known and envied for were their parties, which the whole of Bogotá wanted to attend.

I was very well received that first night, I remember. Pedro introduced me during dinner with a speech so full of praise and compliments about my family that I would soon become a frequent guest of the house. Pedro and Cristina, besides knowing me almost since I was a child (when they still had business with my father in Madrid), were very close to Isabel's parents and they shared the same passions: they were horse riders, compulsive gamblers and music lovers. My relationship with them generated an inexorable trust with Isabel's parents. The following week I would see Isabel again, but this time I was invited directly by her parents, to a piano recital.

But that first night was not only when I met Isabel and her family. It was also when I heard the rumors about her brother, Tomás. An open secret that everyone in town was talking about, but no one had confirmed. Rumors and nothing but rumors, I thought.

People said that Tomás was born with severe malformations and mental retardation. They said that he lived tied up, with chains, in the attic of the house, that beautiful mansion in La Merced with impeccable gardens and imposing trees at the entrance that glorified the neighborhood. It was also said that he would escape at night, to the hills, to Monserrate, where he would catch his victims and tear them to pieces. There were many stories and superstitions I heard about Tomás, but none of them were credible, much less confirmed.

People spoke of Tomás with surprising belligerence. I felt so disgusted to hear it. They spread rumors about him, his parents, and their parties without any modesty or discretion, even in the house itself, while they were their guests and drinking their wines. Leopoldo and Cecilia said, for example, that all these celebrations were more a whim of the father than anything else, to keep his wife Helena (the devoted mother, bound in pain by the suffering of his son), entertained. Mercedes and her sister Nelly, on the other hand, said the parties were more like business meetings (although people said they were going to look for a husband). And then there was Alba, who said that all this was pure banality, something trivial, pure pretension to maintain their status and social profile (They said she was a lesbian).

To me, this circus was very surprising—and only with time could I understand that it was a new form of entertainment, a new post-colonial tableau, perhaps, where the rich seemed to want to imitate the French romanticism of magazines in order to appear more European and less "Creole." Everything was allowed, it seemed, and even the cheapest and most irrelevant rumor was news.

A week after the piano recital, I received another invitation. An American violinist was to give a private dress rehearsal before his concert. The critics were anxious and the young virtuoso's performance was eagerly awaited. I arrived punctually, with some roses, I remember, for Helena. Isabel welcomed me and received the flowers for her mother and gave them to the maid to put them in water. She told me that her mother was attending to the rector of the Lyceum, but that she would be back soon. Then she signaled for me to follow her to the second floor as people gathered in the hall. This had happened before, during the piano recital. I thought it was complete nonsense and I didn't want to repeat it; it was only the third time I had been to that house and I had a very good reputation among the family. Isabel was also much younger than me. Being alone with her was an affront not only to Isabel's parents, but also to the Valenzuela family. I could not imagine if Pedro or Cristina found out about it; it would bring shame and dishonor to their family. I decided to go straight to the living room and have a drink. Away from Isabel, I would be much better off.

That night, there were many people, more than the previously. I was in the hall, next to Altagracia, talking with the priests and teachers of the Lyceum about the kinds of absurd and superfluous topics that arose during these events, when I saw Isabel approaching. She was not giving up. She entered the room and told me that she needed to show me her new literature books. The mother looked askance at the priest, who opted to take his glass of wine and drink, looking away with a smile. I felt quite uncomfortable, but I had no choice but to follow her —to do otherwise would have been unchivalrous and rude. So, I followed her upstairs, and thus we ended up back at the same thing. The flesh is weak, and Isabel was extremely beautiful and fiery. Lost in her kisses, there was no turning back.

LUIS STARES AT THE WINDOW, pensive. It seems as if Isabel had been his love. I wanted to ask more, but I thought it would be a bad time. I stood by, as usual, to let him tell me what he wanted to tell me. In the end, that was what Alicia always asked of me, not to pressure Luis. "What Luis has to tell you, he will tell you," she said.

"But that night, something unexpected happened", Luis continued.

After the intermission, Isabel's father began to call for her emphatically. Isabel came out, alarmed, thinking that her father would find us in that little room, and that he would go crazy. I didn't know what to do, so I decided to wait, in silence, with my heart racing, repentant for what I had done and praying to God to forgive me and perform a miracle.

I waited in that room for a long time. I don't remember how long, but I remember it took forever. There I was, nervous, sweating, like when I used to go with Pablo to the baths in Salamanca, to look at the pictures of naked women that we had collected at Don José's flea market. When I felt that everything was back to normal and there was silence, I decided to leave and pretend that nothing had happened. That was when, in the hallway, I heard a voice coming from behind a door: "Luis, come here," it said. At first I was scared. I thought someone might have seen us. But then I realized that it was Isabel's brother—who else could speak from there? Only that monster everyone was afraid of. The voice discreetly asked me if he could come out into the hallway before the concert was over, to listen better. I said yes, it would be no problem for me, but he told me that I had to go downstairs, otherwise he would not come out. I urged him to come out, and told him that I also wanted to stay hidden for the moment. Tomás replied that he knew why I wanted to be hidden. Then there was silence… And then he opened the door, furtively, and came out—and I was terrified.

There was nothing monstrous about Tomás, though, not a hint of it. On the contrary, he was a good-looking young man with a calm temperament. He did strike me as a little weak, or delicate, but I didn't see the monster that people talked so much about. Tomás was surprised by my reaction. He couldn't seem to understand it. He asked me if everything was all right, and I told him yes, that I was just confused, because I thought Isabel's brother, meaning him, was very sick.

Tomás told me that it was true and that he was sick, but that he could not tell me what it was. Then there was silence again. I told him that I had to go downstairs, and that I hoped he would get better. Then he said to me: "Luis, can I ask you a favor?" I answered yes, knowing that he knew my secret. He told me that he would like me to bring him a bottle of rum, on the sly. Then there was silence again... Then I said goodbye. I remember he added —I am twenty-two years old. I can hold my liquor.

That night I went home thinking about Tomás. What had happened to him? I wondered. Was it something internal? Was he dying of a slow disease? I remember it all seemed very strange to me. But I figured I shouldn't ask, that I should respect Isabel's pain and that of her family.

The following week I met Isabel, just after the twelve o'clock mass, while on my way to the Sunday concert. We were talking a bit when, although I had promised myself that I would not ask anything, I decided to do so, just like that, very unguarded, like Mercedes and Nelly, who deliberately whispered at parties but then pretended to be innocent and oblivious.

I told her that I had something to confess to her—that that night, after the incident with her father, I had met Tomás, by chance, and had found him to be a very nice guy, and that I would like to know what he had. Of course I didn't tell her what people were whispering, although I sensed that she knew, because she was a very smart girl and understood her parents' friendships very well.

Isabel felt uncomfortable, I could also sense that, but she did not hesitate to respond. Once the concert was over, we left together and sat down at the café on Jimenez Avenue, on 4th Street. Isabel began the conversation by saying that this was a subject that neither she nor her family talked about, but since I had met Tomás and I was a foreigner, she would explain what it was all about.

Isabel told me that Tomás had leprosy. He had had it since he was very young, and although it was not so visible, he did have it and it was a reality, and therefore it was the family's responsibility to isolate him and keep him away from others. Isabel felt comfortable with her parents' decision to do so. She supported them. She also told me that Helena, her mother, had had a leprous sister growing up, and this had created great trauma and pain in the family.

Apparently, Elvira, as the aunt was called, had been diagnosed with leprosy at a very young age. The family did not want to denounce her, even though this was a requirement at the time. However, soon after (and apparently as a result of differences with Helena's family), someone secretly denounced Elvira and her parents. The people of the neighborhood, along with the workers on her father's banana farms, marched to their hacienda to ask that the girl be sent to Agua de Dios. Helena's father shed deep tears, while the workers outside the hacienda took justice into their own hands and set fire to the crops and harvest. The next morning, Elvira, now a pariah, entered Agua de Dios. Only Helena and a maid accompanied her.

Months later, Elvira disappeared without trace. Helena never knew what happened, or at least Isabel says she never told. Her father died soon after, hating Colombia and cursing his land.

I was not surprised that Tomás's parents did not want to repeat the story, especially not Helena. Many years had already passed since those concentration camps, but still, in the streets, there fear and shame about them. The stigma haunts us even to this day.

Tomás's look was not the image I had of lepers—I remember this was the first thing I thought after hearing Isabel's confession. Those who were taken prisoner in the white wagon of the train. Those unhappy, poor, wretched people who had no one and who wandered the streets while their skin was falling apart. I thanked Isabel for her trust and promised her I would not say anything.

Then, time passed. I kept my promise to Tomás and brought him the rum. From then on, we made a beautiful friendship, at least until what happened…

(Silence).

"And what happened?" I demand to know.

"I owe the art of writing to Ponceta, and not to Augusto, as many people think," Luis answers abruptly.

"But what happened?" I ask again.

"All this you are hearing, dear Leonardo, is thanks to Ponceta. I am telling you. Listen to me. It is not because of Augusto, as many think. The reason is that all this is written down, otherwise, I wouldn't even remember it now," the old man answers with a grumpy tone.

"I will tell you why," Luis continues.

I liked Ponceta, and when I went to see Augusto I used to talk to her. But what else could you talk to your psychoanalyst's wife about, if not your problems and your therapy? So that—writing about my problems, which Augusto had recommended I do —became an excuse to talk to Ponceta. She said that I could share everything I wrote with her if I ever needed a listening ear other than the psychoanalyst, and I, for my part, chose to listen to her. So I began to write. I was writing for Ponceta. That is the truth, my dear Leonardo.

Since that day I have written about everything, and as the years went by, the habit became a vice. Ponceta is no longer here… (Only in my thoughts, of course) but writing never left my side and it is thanks to this that today I can remember everything I am telling you: about Isabel, about Helena, and about Tomás.

We were barely in the third session when Augusto told me to write. I was not yet able to share with him all the disconcerting feelings I had stuck in my chest. Augusto told me that I needed to sit down to write and face, so to speak, the anguish of the past. To revisit those painful memories of childhood and youth that I was so afraid of.

That day, after crying and crying, as had become my habit, Augusto would tell me something I would never forget: You can't go through life avoiding the past, he told me. And he was right. Oh, so right.

Augusto said that the exercise of writing would help me to face that other painful self and ensure that my future would be strengthened without resentment. I never agreed. Contrary to what Augusto said, I knew that sooner or later this exercise would become a burden to me; I told him so that very day as we ate lunch after the session. But Augusto was a stubborn and impatient man, and besides being my therapist, he was a great friend—so I, foolishly I suppose, ended up listening to him.

To be honest, I didn't like the methods Augusto used with his patients. He insisted however, that they worked, and that at least with several of his patients, who were mostly displaced from the war (some had even been in Auschwitz), the methods suited them very well. Ponceta didn't believe much in it either, and sometimes she would tell me, when I went to dinner at his house, to just follow the lead, to tell him that everything was fine and that the treatment was working.

Many, many years have passed since that exercise. I have thrown many pages into the fireplace; other things I have kept, and many others… are here. The exercise of writing—and Augusto was right about this—brings you, more than the experience of remembering and resolution, an inexplicable sensation of calm. And maybe, perhaps, that is why it becomes a positive exercise. I'm not saying pleasant, much less comfortable. Just positive, I think… although we could argue about that too.

(Silence).

LUIS SAT AT HIS DESK, and I didn't know what to do. This was a situation I was not used to. I kept looking at the door, thinking that Alicia might come in, and help me re-direct the old man. I couldn't find coherence in the stories, and it would be very difficult to write something sensible with so much information from so many different times and moments.

"Well, this is perhaps the ninth time I have reviewed this writing this week," says Luis. Twelve in total this month, five last month, and I think that before the summer I had already read it a couple of times more; I must have the annotations in a drawer somewhere, to be more precise. Whenever I revisit it,

I always say the same thing: I will not read it again. I will not read it again. That's the way it is, and the fact is that whenever I read it, I always find things that hurt me, and when I find them, I start to get upset and then, I want to send it all to hell. These writings come from different moments, from different feelings. Some are still from that time, when I was young and with a lot of resentment inside. Others are the same, but revisited in my adult years. They are more compassionate, more mature… Reading them all, it's like tearing off pieces of skin with a razor blade over and over again in the same wound. You go back and forth, and then you not only visit that past, but also those moments when you wrote this or that. You end up multiplying again and again the same story, and all of them in the end belong to that same hate you carry inside; but as Alicia says, the time has come to end it all, and whether it is for good or for bad (I hope it is better than bad), I will end this chapter. I understand that I must do it, that I must put everything in order and have everything ready for the interview. But all this scares me a lot and gives me reason, moreover, to confirm that Augusto was not right, and that all this exercise of writing has not brought me any light, nor any peace of mind, nor even any bullshit. Only the joy that Ponceta gave me. Nothing more. And

Ponceta is no longer here, so I don't understand why I should continue writing.

"Calm down, Luis," I told him. "There is no need to talk about it, if it bothers you."

"I will talk about whatever I want to talk about," Luis replied angrily.

"Very well," I told him. "The important thing is that you are well."

(Silence).

Alicia says that perfection has been my greatest virtue, but I tell her that more than a virtue, it has been a horrible whip, like those that Father Eusebio gave you to flagellate your sins and your lust. I recognize that more than a perfectionist I have become obsessive and stubborn with things. With everything. Music seem to me poorly recorded, most singers seem to me mediocre; writings like this one, garbage, and cinema, heaven forbid. Alicia says that I'm old, tired, and full of traumas and pains as a child, and that's why now that I'm beginning to return, so to speak, to that childhood to which we all have to return, all these whims come to the surface. I don't know, it's as if I simply can't control them.

"Luis, we can continue tomorrow, I told him.

"It's already a little late and you must be tired."

"Are you tired?" asks the old man angrily.

"Because I am not."

"No, I'm not, but you look uncomfortable."

"Well, to tell you the truth, it's been a long time since I've felt as anxious as I do today," Luis answers. The last time I remember feeling something similar was when I left Paris and returned to Spain, and that's a long time ago… I think my father had already died, if memory serves me correctly. At that time, I remember, I felt the same as I do today: hopelessness, incomprehension, a certain shame and anxiety, and a lot of loneliness, a lot of it…

(Silence).

It is useless to think that we can go back to the beginning of everything without feeling that we are throwing ourselves into a fatuous and desolate void that devours you in the attempt. The rush of time has changed considerably. As I feel and perceive it now, it is not as it was before. The rush of time also gets old and tired. The notion of time is ephemeral, says

Alicia, when she goes out into the garden to water the roses.

I, for a long time now, have not been in a hurry for anything. I prefer to live between pauses and the passing of the hours and the passing of silence. It is better that time does not even stop. So I can look him in the eyes and ask for accountability.

"And what are you afraid of?" I asked.

"A lot," Luis answers. "Although it may not seem like it, I have a lot to fear."

And no, I am not ungrateful, as Alicia tells me, and she knows I resent her saying so. But not everything in life is about money. Maybe when you don't have it, you think that's the main thing, but when you have it, you realize that it doesn't contribute anything to happiness. Just false comfort. I don't want to sound like an old man giving advice on self-improvement, far from it, but the truth is, that's the way it is. Plainly, that's how it is.

(Silence).

But I'm so tired… I'm so tired of fearing and waiting. Not sleeping well at night, the next day I'm exhausted, and this makes me spend the day upset and angry. Alicia worries, but I tell her that I'm not sleeping because of the cold weather in Bogotá these days, although we both know I'm lying. She doesn't tell me, but I know she knows. Last week she brought me some beautiful flowers from the garden and we talked. I love the flowers Alicia grows; they are beautiful.

Alicia asked me why I was so anxious, and I remember her telling me that the interview thing was irrelevant. The pain was already done, she told me. There was no way there could be any more pain. That sentence left me thoughtful. Alicia sometimes seems a bit indelicate, but the truth is that she is not. It's no wonder I've been living with her most of my life. She couldn't be indelicate I thought.

Maybe I'm losing my mind, I think. And why not? I have the right to do so. In the end, our minds also grow old and tired, like hours, like time. Maybe mine doesn't even want to remember anymore. Maybe I'm just making it up, as usual, to satisfy that compulsive feeling that this life was really worth it. Could it be?

(Silence).

Luis becomes pensive again, as he listens to his thoughts in his head:

ALICIA TOLD ME that the journalist was a young man. I think he was in his early thirties or thereabouts. I'm anxious about whether we'll be able to talk peacefully. Today's youth is in such a hurry with everything, I can't stand it. Besides, they are uneducated. There is no formation, no manners. They don't know what the world is about. They just want to party and fuck without knowing anything. And no, I'm not a prude. I also liked to fuck. Even at this age, I still sneak into Alicia's room and grope her.

Alicia, on the contrary, says that I should trust the young people, that they are the future. That I should understand that they go at a different speed, but that doesn't mean they are bad. And that is true. On the other hand, there is something, which I have not confessed to Alicia, but I will confess now—and it is that sharing this story with someone young gives me less anxiety and calms my spirit. Not much! I mean, not too much… Just a little bit…

I asked Alicia how I should start: Deep, honest, upset? I don't know how to share this with someone I don't know. And I know it may not be anything extraordinary enough to keep in such suspense. But it's my privacy. My past. My childhood, my dreams, my frustrations. And that already makes it so, so complicated for me. Even now, I'm starting to shake and feel nervous. I think I'll have a scotch, although Alicia won't let me. I'll do it quietly, and it'll be neat, so Alicia won't notice…

(Silence).

Fuck!, why can't I pour myself a drink in my own house… why do I have to ask for Alicia's permission?

(Silence).

Well, Alicia is very complicated, and I don't want to argue with her. No. Especially now, when I'm feeling so vulnerable. But let's get back to the interview, the guy is looking at me with a funny face.

Alicia has suggested that I should start at the beginning and speak about my Salamanca days. But what memories of Salamanca do I have? Oh yes, one or two: the nuns, of course, the piano. Also the halls and the winter. The solitude. The river Tormes. The old mill. My God! I remember so much. Maybe I should start only from Madrid. Or maybe I should just stay within the quotation marks? Just answer what the boy asks me. Maybe it's all so superfluous and banal, and here I am tormenting myself for something that won't even happen. Maybe I should smoke a joint, behind Alicia's back, in the tower…

(Silence).

(Again doing something on the sly…)

Lately I have been thinking a lot about Pablo. What became of him? I have many memories with Pablo. The first time I masturbated, it was with him, watching Sister Esther bathing in the pond. He was also the first one I smoked with, and that's not to mention that he was the first one with whom I spent a punishment in the wells of the orphanage, after taking some communion wafers out of the sacristy and eating them with strawberry jam. What memories…

(Silence).

A couple of years ago I visited Salamanca. Did I tell you? I was with Alicia, in Madrid, visiting Carmen and Claridad. We were going to the Santander film festival, so on our way to the north, we decided to stop there first in the city. Alicia did not know Salamanca, so I thought would be nice to take her to the school and to the places I liked, although, of course, there was not much left of most of them.

When we arrived, the first thing I thought, standing there, was how fast time had gone by. I was old, exhausted, and humorless, but in front of me, there was the school, as if nothing had happened, slender and robust, although, of course, much had happened and I knew it.

(Silence).

"Luis, are you all right? You're speechless…"

"Where were we?" Luis asked.

"I don't know," I answered. "I really don't know."

"And then all those notebooks and notes? I thought they were precisely for taking notes. Alicia said you were a good journalist, but the truth is I don't believe it…

(Silence).

But very well, I'll tell you about when I found out the truth and please take note of it," said Luis, a little annoyed.

When I learned the truth, I thought I would never be the same. I thought that the truth I had discovered would haunt me forever, silent and lying in wait, and that it would try to harm me, as if it carried in its shadow a Machiavellian being ready to kill us all. It was not like that, of that I am sure. The only Machiavellian beings with a thirst for revenge are ourselves. The shadows in the end are only a pale reflection of our decadence and limitation.

That afternoon has never left my mind. I remember the trembling voice of that sick old man—an old man with a sad and lost look, with interminable frustration. I don't know why I thought priests lived in harmony, full of God and happiness, as my mother used to say. That day, my image of them changed. It is useless to think that we can go back to the beginning of everything without feeling that we are throwing ourselves into a fatuous and desolate void that devours you in the attempt. It is useless to think that everything will always return to its cause. It is useless to think. It is useless to remember. Death is perhaps the only hope of existence, and with it, we cling to life. The hope of having hope. It is contrast…

(Silence).

When Alicia shared her idea with me, my first thought was to go to the bathroom. The bathroom is the only place in this house where I have solitude, at least for now—and the study, although Alicia also enters there as master and mistress. The first thing I told her was that I didn't think it was a good idea to tell a journalist my most intimate secrets. I thought that my past and my nostalgia belonged only to me. To no one else. But then, Alicia reminded me of Augusto's words: *"You can't go through life avoiding the past..."*

My mind is so restless that I have to try to calm it down again. It constantly evokes a skeptical internal dialogue that asks me thousands of questions, that makes me doubt so many things, that forces me to intervene, control my thoughts, and silence the uncertainty—which is not easy. Fortunately, after replying or answering my own questions, brimming with fear, I manage to calm down and repeat to myself that it is the right thing to do, that I must reveal it, that I must free myself from that chain of silence that I imposed on myself. If this were not the case, perhaps I would have run away by now.

What should I do? Go to bed? Call Alicia to come and keep me company? Will her presence calm me down? How long until nightfall?

I am struggling so much with myself that maybe, and just maybe, I ended up missing it. I had ceased to be aware of my surroundings…

(Silence).

…Where was I? Oh yes, on Alicia and her idea… What was she saying? I don't remember anymore. Was it something from the past? Was it something scary that I don't want to remember? I don't have the strength for this…

I fix my eyes on the sky again and notice that the sun is indeed setting and I wasn't even noticing it. I almost missed it, but fortunately I did not. Again, the majesty of the universe comes to my rescue and brings me some peace. It quiets my head for a moment, as I like to say.

But then something caresses my face. I take my hand and the creature moves a little away. I realize that it is a sky-blue butterfly when I take a good look at it. I remember someone once told me that these pretty creatures are actually good souls who sometimes wander among the living just to bring them a little beauty and joy. Right? Is that a lie? Is it death that has come? Then maybe I should run and tell everything, because I don't want to die with this anguish and with this secret. But the journalist will not come until Tuesday, Alicia told me. Is today Tuesday? Has he already been here? Where is my calendar?…

Oh! Dear mother, why do you always change things around?

The butterfly is fluttering, it stumbles against the window pane again and again. I want to let it out, I don't want it to get hurt, I want it to be free like me, although I can't really be free anymore because of my worn-out body and cracked soul. I try to open the window, but my strength falters. I find I cannot. I think the butterfly will die. And that was enough. I had somehow kept myself whole, but just barely. That was enough for me to collapse, to collapse. I did, I collapsed, like a house of cards succumbing to the innocent breath of a child.

My legs faltered so I dropped to my knees, coinciding with the sunset. That was it. I let myself fall into the gloom and darkness. The twilight of a man. Will I finally be consumed?

My chest hurts, my heart has fluttered again, I can barely breathe. Is it the end? Is my heart refusing to work? Is it tired of carrying so much on its back? I can't die now; I haven't told anyone yet. The worst thing a human being can do to himself is to die with regret in his heart. I realize that one certainly regrets what one does not do, but what you do never comes to that cruel denouement. Hold on Luis. You must be able to do it. You have to be here, to be able to speak.

Then and only then do I recognize the symptoms and realize that I am not dying. I am having a panic attack. It's not the first one I've had, but the first one in a long, long time. I try to control my breathing. Once again I resolve not to let my mind win because what is a panic attack but your mind attacking you? There is no turning back. Alicia convinced me and I agreed. I can't just take it back. This is what I have to do. What, perhaps, I should have done a long time ago. Sure, I'm too scared and I feel less than ready. But, I don't think I'll ever feel ready. If not now, then never. How could I be proud to take the secret to my grave? I couldn't. Bare your soul, the diary tells me. I must bare my soul when I talk to the journalist and that's not what really worries me—it's not him, it's that the world will find out everything. Will I manage to do it? Can a human being ever be more vulnerable than in a situation like this? Don't we usually get defensive and try everything so that others don't realize our vulnerability? And I am going to make mine visible, to shatter my protective shell that for years I tried so hard to erect.

I must wash my face and clear my mind. I have to, before I suffer any more breakdowns.

"They will know. Pretty soon everyone will know and it will be you who is going to tell them…"

Where did that come from? My inner voice talking to me again? My mind echoing my doubts and uncertainty. Or was it you, diary?

I remember the blue butterfly—I had forgotten it. I look for it with my eyes, as if frantic. I turn my face towards it so fast that my neck hurts. It's still there, banging against the glass, trying to get out, it won't give up. That beautiful creature will get hurt and I don't want to witness it so I get up with my whole body trembling and start pulling again on the window, wanting to help her, to set her free… Is my little physical strength gone along with the little emotional strength I have left? “What are you doing?” I hear. A honeyed voice caresses my ears, it comes from the door of the study that had been closed and is now half-open. It is Alicia, who looks at me from the threshold with big eyes, very big shocked eyes. Is it so late? Has Alicia come to light the embers already? Before I can say anything she is already beside me and helps me to sit up. Which I do with difficulty. She leads me to the chair I woke up in minutes before, or was it hours? How long have I been struggling?

Alicia accompanies my recovery with a sweet and soft scent. It is not perfume. It is something subtler. Only then do I realize that Alicia was carrying beautiful flowers in her arms—flowers of vivid colors. I had mentioned to her that I felt like having flowers in my studio because they would help inspire me when writing something special I had had in mind. She remembered and went to get them. Alicia, sweet Alicia! Her thoughtfulness eases my tension.

“What happened?” she asks in an alarmed voice and makes me remember the state in which she found me.

I want to explain myself coherently. To tell her everything from the beginning, from the nightmare, my inner doubts, the collapse. But I just say: "The butterfly. The butterfly…"

I babble while I look for it with my eyes all over the place. It's not there, it didn't seem to be there, there's no trace of it…

(Silence).

Had it left the studio?

"There is nothing, Luis. There's no butterfly here", Alicia says. "I think you have to rest. Tomorrow, if you want, you can explain to me what happened."

I'm so tempted to tell her that, no, I don't want to rest!, that I can't rest—but I leave it at that. Instead, I let her help me to the bed.

I am greeted by her softness, the smell of clean blankets… my room. Alicia unwraps the blankets for me and helps me to lie down. Then she tucks them around me. It feels good, it feels warm. I'm tired, I murmur. I've slept, but I'm so tired… What if that butterfly was just a reflection of my mind making me more aware that I need freedom?

"Will I ever be able to fly free like that beautiful butterfly?" I ask out loud but the question is not directed at anyone.

(Silence).

Alicia is looking at me with a strange gleam in her eyes. Very strange.

Before I can be aware of anything else, I am once again asleep again. I find myself plunged into complete darkness, but accompanied by them, my memories, the music, and the Maestro's piano, playing through that pink window on those hot June days.

LEONARDO REMAINS THOUGHTFUL and turns off the recorder. The sound attracts Luis's attention.

"What are you doing?" Luis asks. "Are you leaving already?"

"Yes, I think we're done for the day," Leonardo answers.

"Where were we going? I'm sorry I got distracted looking at that butterfly in the garden," says Luis, as he looks at the window with difficulty.

"No need to apologize," says Leonardo. "It's been a great talk. We'll continue tomorrow."

(Silence).

"By the way, Leonardo, and before you go," says Luis, turning his gaze back to the window:

"That was the first time I saw a leper. It was at a dinner party, at Isabel's house. I don't know if I told you about her… she was one of my great youthful loves," says Luis, leaving the studio slowly, supported by his cane and his memories.

(Silence).

2
Luis & Leonardo

Conversations with Luis always ended in unexpected and annoying monologues, the kind that appear and cross the space of what is not said, what is not whispered. Pensive between his books and his music, he resorted to oblivion as his only abiding weapon to defend his madness and his pride. Time does not exist in his space; neither do his words. The octogenarian man is leisurely. He is in no hurry and has no path. His gaze is empty and dense (like his monologues), unexpected and silent.

I listen to Bach's music while Luis writes. The light from the fireplace recreates his figure on the ceiling of the studio. The place is spacious, with large windows covered by thick curtains. On the right side of the desk, on a cushion, is his cat: he is twelve years old. Like his owner, he looks tired. Alicia says he can't see anymore and that he will have to be put to sleep soon. At the back of the studio is a grand piano. On top of the instrument there are scores of photos: one in Paris, one with Alicia, and one of a boy with a nun. I guess that's him. At the entrance of the studio, on the right side, there is a huge library full of books, records, and antique collection carts. Next to the piano is a green leather sofa, and to one side of the sofa, a table. Behind the sofa there is a painting; it looks like a charcoal drawing. Luis has his back turned, concentrating on his writing.

I approach slowly, without making any noise, trying not to let him feel my presence:

IT IS 11:24 P.M. on any given day. The music evokes the images of a movie whose premiere, in a theater in Rome, reminds me of loneliness. The fireplace is lit. Every evening, at eight o'clock, Alicia lights it. Now I sit writing, remembering and inventing a story. A light dew falls on the window to my left. The night seems to want to be silent. Neither can the wind be heard.

The image of the clock takes me to the old bell tower of Agua de Dios. It is 3:30 in the morning. The plaza is empty. I see nothing but the lights in the security sentry boxes around town. Someone comes out of one of the corners of the square. The music continues mysteriously, intertwined with the sounds of crickets and the movement of the trees.

(Silence).

Luis continues writing:

I hear a voice again and then the clock. Life is like a clock. A clock that marks the hours: the time of arrival and the time of departure. The hours that remind us of the end. The endings that do not forget. The hours, slow and leisurely, also have an end…

(Silence).

The footsteps of the Mother Director are heard. I know it is her because I recognize that sound. I am waiting in her office because we need to talk. Sister Esther has told me she has something to tell me. I am frightened by the picture of St. Ignatius behind her desk. It has always frightened me. I like the way he looks in the books Sister Esther reads to us better. The chair is high and my feet are dangling. My sweaty hands are on my knees.

"Are you happy?" asks the Mother Director.

"Yes, mother," Luis answers quietly.

The Mother Director places her hands on little Luis's file:

"I want you to pack your suitcase with all your things. Say goodbye to Sister Esther and come back here. Don't say goodbye to Pablo or any of your classmates. They don't know yet."

Luis nods his head. He gets up and goes to the door. He opens it, staring at the superior. He asks her:

"Mother, do you think my parents will be happy?"

"Of course, Luis," she answers, "Ignacio and Blanca are extraordinary people, and they will give you a lot of love. Your parents will be very happy with your new family."

Luis smiles and closes the door. The Mother Director remains thoughtful.

(Silence).

In my younger years I considered that the past was not part of my life. I lived in the San Ignacio orphanage until I was ten years old, when the Muñoz family adopted me. I grew up in Madrid, always accompanied by a vague feeling of abandonment and loneliness.

My life has been more than eighty years of constant struggle with myself. You are the inevitable result of your time and your experiences. You know your limitations and you learn to live with the disappointment of accepting your fragile vulnerability. You also learn to live with your fears, with the inconsolable misfortune that makes you stronger or weaker. What was once a torment, with old age, becomes peace of mind. Too late, I think, for anything but destinies and designs, little or nothing can be changed.

I remember Salamanca with deep nostalgia. I remember its small streets, crowded with people, when the processions passed by during Holy Week. I remember its ochre fields and those big birds that always amazed me, perched on the roofs of the churches. I remember the cakes of María, the Dominican, that we ate while we went for a walk on Saturdays along the river. I remember the swimming pool in the winters.

I remember the smell of my freshly laundered sheets, Mother Director's breath, the cherry toothpaste that Doña Martha would send us, and Sister Genoveva's buttered robe. I also remember the smell of pine and old cedar from the piano, and the smell of incense from the small chapel.

San Ignacio was one of the oldest orphanages in Spain at the time. It had formerly been a novitiate house of the Jesuit Fathers; but, in time, and after having been closed for a long period, it passed into the hands of the local government. Soon after, it became what I knew: a gloomy and sad orphanage.

My first years of life were confusing. Memories of that time are associated with music. I dreamed of a place I had never visited, but where I heard music that was familiar to me. That music gave me peace of mind. It was like a feeling of belonging and of home. Then I would wake up, calm, with the tune still in my head, but disturbed and restless, wishing to know more.

"Luis, Luis!" the Mother Director shouted like crazy when the firewood was extinguished.

It didn't matter where she was or what time it was. The important thing was to keep warm inside the mother's office.

"Here I am! I'm on my way! I'm on my way!" I shouted at the top of my lungs as I ran back and forth through the wide corridors that separated the dormitories from the cloisters and the Sisters' offices.

"I've already told you not to let the fireplace go out," said the Mother Director, as she scrubbed her hands vigorously.

Life in the orphanage was modest and simple. We all slept together in a small room with a fireplace in the center, four beds on one side and five on the other. Next to it were the showers, divided into two parts, one for boys and one for girls. On the second floor we had the dining room, with two tables, a small one where the nuns sat, and a big one for us. Leaving the dining room we entered the chapel, small and austere. The figure of a small saint was the only thing that adorned it. Then there was the library, on the other side of the chapel, also small (I can assure you that it had no more than twenty books). At the back of the building was the kitchen, large and cool. And finally, there was the garden, next to the kitchen. It had a court, a pond, and a fountain.

The little we learned in the orphanage was thanks to the nuns, because we had no formal education. Some teachers came once or twice a month, but it was the nuns who contributed the most to our education.

The orphanage had very few benefactors. The money they sent us was barely enough for the weekly shopping. The neighbors in town helped us. They sent food, clothes, and school supplies, but even this was not enough. The Mother Director fought tirelessly to keep the orphanage going, but we all lived under the constant threat that one day it would be closed and we would be thrown out on the street.

In an orphanage you learn to appreciate what it means to have a family. Although we came from different places and situations, all of us who lived there shared the same feeling of abandonment. The orphanage was the only thing we had, and although its comforts were modest, it provided us with the most important thing, what we needed most: the love and warmth of a family.

Day to day life was full of rules and schedules.
At 5:50 in the morning we would get up and head for the showers. Then we would return to the dormitory, make our beds, get dressed in uniform and go down to the chapel. At 6:30 we would begin the first prayers, led by the Mother Director. Then followed the mass (if the priest was present that day) and then we would go to the dining room for breakfast.

Classes lasted all morning. At eleven o'clock we had a snack and a short twenty-minute break. Then we had an hour that we used, depending on the day, for physical education, music, handicrafts, or for gathering dictated by the Mother Director. Painting, dance, and theater were led by Sister Genoveva. Piano, guitar, and flute were taught by Sister Esther, while sewing and handicrafts were taught by the Mother Director. Physical education was led by Don José.

At one o'clock we had lunch, in silence, listening to one of us recite the lives and virtues of the saints. At 1:45 we had a short break and at two o'clock we went back to class. By 4:30 we would begin our chores. I had to work in the laundry and in the library. Then at six o'clock we had prayers again, which were followed by a meditation led by Sister Genoveva. Then we had another break and later dinner, also in silence, but this time listening to passages from the Gospels. We ended the day with the last prayers and then went to sleep in absolute silence.

On weekends the schedule changed. On Saturdays we had walks, the sites of which rotated every eight days. Sometimes we went to the river, sometimes to the forest, and sometimes to the olive groves. My favorite place was the river. Pablo and I had discovered a house there with a water mill that we called the *old mill.* The shack was about an hour from the orphanage, in the middle of a dense forest, on the banks of the Tormes River. It was a small wooden house, abandoned, with a water mill inside that no longer worked. We had found some boards nearby and used them as a bridge to get inside. There we ate, played cards, and took naps.

We took many trips to the old mill. I always wanted to return to it, but time did not give me the opportunity to do so. The mill reminds me of the Salamanca seasons and, perhaps for that reason, its memory has a physical nuance. The winters of that time were very cold and the summers very hot. But in the mill, when it was winter, the shack gave us warmth, and if it was summer, it gave us coolness. After walking for an hour under the summer sun, there was nothing better than going into the river and then taking a delicious siesta.

On Sundays I remember the Mass in the cathedral, the confessions with Father Jesús, and the walks in the central square. I also remember the concerts of the Sisters in the afternoon (always with the same songs), and the lunch menu, which never changed. I remember Sister Genoveva's voice interpreting some well-known aria, accompanied by Sister Esther's piano. The tambourine of the Mother Director, sometimes a little arrhythmic, but always very amusing and the poetry of Don José, tirelessly repeated: *The seminarian of the black eyes.*

Once the weekend was over, it was back to the routine… the waiting… the slow hours…

Time passed, the one that does not forgive, the one that judges. That time, authoritarian and unkind to its innocent visitors, observes quietly, in silence.

A WOMAN RUNS barefoot through one of the streets of the village. I think it is the same figure that has come out of the square. Her feet are bloody. Bach's music continues as Luis Antonio reads aloud from his writing:

The sounds of the mysterious woman's heart grow louder and louder. I don't understand if they are only hers or if they are intertwined with mine. The woman comes to a bridge. I cannot see her face. She cries inconsolably. With difficulty she climbs the railing of the bridge and, opening her arms, she throws herself into the void.

Before the woman falls into the river, Luis Antonio awakens abruptly. He calls Alicia while trying to turn on the light. He is sweating and choking. Alicia wakes up frightened, turns on the light, and looks for her glasses. She walks agitated down the hallway. She opens the doors to Luis's room and rushes in.

"Here I am!" Alicia answers, while she takes a handkerchief and wipes Luis Antonio's sweat.

"Open the safe," Luis tells her in a weak tone.

Alicia approaches the library in the room; she opens the doors at the bottom and begins to take out books. At the bottom is the safe. Trying to remember her password out loud, Alicia opens it in a hurry. Luis's wailing is heard, which makes Alicia even more desperate.

"What do I do, Luis? What do I take?" asks Alicia in despair, shaking her hands and shuffling through the contents.

"The folder, Alicia, the leather folder," answers Luis.

Alicia takes the folder and approaches the bed.

"This is my will, Alicia. Here are all the sleepless hours. It is the story of many and the story of my life. Make it heard, in memory of those who suffered in silence."

"Luis, please, this is just another panic attack. Breathe slowly with me. I'm going to call the doctor now," she replies.

"Don't be silly, Alicia, and take care of Bach. I love you," whispers Luis. *"I don't think two people can be happier than we were."*

Luis closes his eyes slowly, while he caresses Alicia's hand.

Alicia mourns inconsolably the death of her great and only love. Her hand is still clinging to Luis's. After some time, she is petrifying at the window, looking perhaps for an answer...

ALICIA'S TEARS FADE in her thoughts. Sitting in a theater, she listens to the orchestra that has just finished rehearsal, and to the film Director who has cut the scene. Alicia is undaunted, contemplating the distance, just as she did the day Luis died. The sound of the instruments brings her back to her senses. She opens her purse and takes out a handkerchief; she wipes her face and glasses. She holds the folder Luis left her on her lap. She gets up from her chair and walks hurriedly. She leaves the theater and heads for the dressing rooms. The hall is long and dim. She watches the instruments around her. She arrives at the main dressing room and goes through the motions of formality…

"I TOOK MY FIRST piano lessons with Sister Esther," continued Luis.

They were on Tuesdays, on the old and out-of-tune piano in the multi-purpose room. I still remember its dense and penetrating smell, its yellow keys, marked with the fingers of its history, and that dark and deep sound that roared when it was played. It was an antique, upright, large, cabinet-like piano. It was covered by a green blanket that fell to the floor. Sister Esther had knitted it, and she had also made a small one for the chair, which, by the way, was lamé.

That hour of class was very special to me. Sister Esther taught me everything she had learned in the convent during her formative years. I had an enormous passion for music and for the piano in particular. Its sound was close and familiar to me, as if I had it from before, as if it existed from other lives. In the afternoon breaks I would sneak in to play it. I would sit down and begin to imitate everything I saw Sister Esther do.

I admit that, contrary to what my classmates said, my life in the orphanage was not boring. It was sad and lonely, but not boring. I enjoyed my classmates, the Sisters, the daily routine. I enjoyed the walks, the classes, and the sports. I was grateful to everyone, to a family who had opened their doors to me, who loved me, cared for me, and gave me affection.

On long winter nights I had a hard time sleeping. It was quite cold and I had terrible dreams that almost always repeated themselves. I dreamed of a boy walking with someone down a street. They both sit on the sidewalk and listen attentively to the music coming out of an open pink window. I did not understand the reason for the recurrence of the dream nor its meaning. I woke up confused and anxious and then I chose to pray. Who was the child? I wondered. Was it me, perhaps? And if it was me, where was I and who was with me? The realism of those dreams made me think of my parents and the family I should have had. Life in an orphanage constantly confronts you with your past and asks you questions that you don't want to answer.

It was very sad and painful to know so little about my past. The only thing I knew about my parents was what Sister Esther and the Mother Director had told me. They said that they had abandoned me one night on a farm near the village and that I ended up at the door of the orphanage thanks to some farmers who picked me up and took me there. I grew up, then, believing that *God's infinite mercy* was so great that He had sent those people so that, with their kindness and charity, they would take me to the doors of the orphanage and not let me die. Those noble farmers, who were apparently natives of Portugal, had taken me in during the first days after my abandonment. They were on the verge of keeping me, Sister Esther told me, but the poverty in which they lived, their many children, and their desire to leave Salamanca soon made them forget the idea.

That is how I ended up at the doors of San Ignacio and how my spirit and heart grew with a feeling of abandonment, sadness, and incomprehension. Only the piano, and with it, music, could ease my pain and help me understand the unkindness of people and the deep deception I was exposed to since birth. I never knew why (at least at that time), but my love for that sturdy old device was becoming more and more endearing.

3
The Muñoz-Gómez Family

The frustrated life of the Muñoz-Gómez family was known throughout Madrid society. People whispered about Blanca's sadness and about all the experiments she had undergone for the sole purpose of having a child. Among the halls of the orphanage, rumors of her visit began to spread.

None of us knew when it would happen, but when the rumor started, things began to occur that were out of the ordinary. Doña Martha, benefactor of our orphanage, had arrived with a van full of gifts—something that only happened for the Reyes holiday. Our behavior and civility classes grew more intense; housework took longer than usual; the lawns were mowed; the virgins were dressed; and even the fountain at the entrance was washed and stripped of its tenants, the toads, to look clean and decent.

One of those nights I left Pablo a note in his prayer manual. We were ending the day in front of the image of Our Lady, as we used to do every night, when, using signs, I told him to look at the note. We met for a while on the terrace of the chapel while everyone was asleep. I felt that something would happen with the visit of the Muñoz-Gómez family, and I needed to share that feeling with him. It was strange when Pablo told me that it was clear to him that it was time for me to leave the orphanage. My heart had told me so and now Pablo was confirming that premonition.

It was several days before the Mother Director told us what was going on. We could all imagine, but as time went on we chose to think that the rumors had been just that: rumors. However, we were wrong. The visit of the Muñoz-Gómez family was a reality, and it was scheduled for Saturday morning, the 4th.

At that time, the orphanage had nine children. In the time I lived there, I had witnessed only two adoptions. The statistics were not very encouraging.

When Saturday came, we had a big meal and everyone prepared what they did best. There were painting exhibitions, a poetry recital, and sports, and I even had the opportunity to play the piano myself.

I remember that I played some pieces that I had been working with Sister Esther for the annual Christmas concert. The repertoire included Beethoven's well-known *Für Elise*, some small pieces by Schumann, and a very beautiful and simple piece whose composer was unknown. Sister Esther called it *The Wanderer*. I never imagined that this work would mark the rest of my life, and that in that innocent recital would be the beginning of a new future and the end of a dark and hostile past.

When I sat down at the piano I felt like my heart was going to burst. My notes completely blurred. In the reflection of the piano I could see the displeased face of the Mother Director, frowning in annoyance. I did what I could, I remember. But the recital was a disaster. My sense of loss came over me again as it had on those long winter nights. I felt that my possible future with the Muñoz-Gómez family was falling apart, and with it all my hopes and illusions.

When I was about to begin the last piece of the program, that is, *The Wanderer*, I noticed how Sister Esther's cheek shone because of a small and subtle tear. That tear, I only understood many years later, was the last breath to try to finish a program that was already over.

Among the rumors that circulated, besides the talk about how much money the Muñoz-Gómez family had, there was talk of how much they liked and knew about music, something that disturbed me to remember when I sat at the piano. The recital and the visit ended, and several days passed without any news. The tension dropped. No one knew what had happened, but it was strange that right after that visit none of us had left.

But it happened one morning. Salamanca was covered with a diaphanous snow when Sister Esther called me and told me that the Mother Director was waiting for me in her office. I was so astonished that I insistently asked her to tell me what it was all about. The visit to the office only happened when one of us committed a serious offense, or when it was about firewood, something that wasn't possible in this case, since the day before she had filled the baskets with several logs from the forest.

I went to the bathroom to get organized and brush my teeth. I was nervous as I walked through the cold halls leading to the principal's office. When I entered I found her sitting by the fireplace. She was eating a chocolate. Cigarette smoke choked the room and a chill made my teeth chatter. Mother asked me to sit next to her in the chair next to her. We stared at each other as I inhaled the smoke coming out of her mouth. She offered me a chocolate, but I said no.

She asked me what my classmates were saying about the Muñoz-Gómez visit. I answered that and other questions with a tone of feigned astonishment and ignorance. Then she pulled out a letter she had crumpled in her pocket and gave it to me to read. I began reading in my mind. She instructed me to do it out loud.

The sound of burning firewood served as a background to understand what I was reading. The Muñoz-Gómez family was sending a letter of request. In it they requested authorization to adopt young Luis, who had enchanted Doña Blanca so much with his piano. I could not understand it. It was as if God had finally remembered me. I hugged the Mother Director and immediately ran to tell Sister Esther the news.

When I closed the door of the Mother Director's office my heart was pounding so hard that I felt like I was suffocating. My little legs trembled with every step. I was torn between two fears, a before and an after. That orphanage was my home, and to leave it now was like leaving a part of myself.

I went with a certain resignation, disguised as joy, to dear Sister Esther's room. I knocked on her door and passed in silence. We looked at each other, hugged each other, and between many tears we said goodbye. Then she went to her bedside table, opened a small drawer, took out the music score and handed it to me. She said that the score had been the architect of recovering what destiny had taken away from me: my family.

The next day, the Mother Director came to my room and asked me to be ready by ten o'clock in the morning. She also told me not to say goodbye to any of my classmates. Filled with joy and nostalgia, I put in a small suitcase what little clothes I had, along with the illusion of starting a new life where there would no longer be room for fears and frustrations.

As requested by the Mother Director, I left the orphanage with only a goodbye to Sister Esther. I did not even have the courage to disobey the Mother Director and say goodbye to Pablo, my great friend and companion in my adventures.

The Muñoz-Gómez family's chauffeur arrived in fifteen minutes, which seemed like an eternity to me. Sitting on the fountain, with a small suitcase on my knees, wearing my dark blue shorts and my Havana sweater knitted by Sister Esther, I said goodbye to the Salamanca landscapes. I gazed at the dome of the cathedral with nostalgia and lowered my head with humility.

The trip was long. Although I had never left Salamanca, I knew that Madrid was not far away.

"What a long trip! Modesto, I thought Madrid was nearer," I said to the driver in a tired tone, while I was cleaning the car window.

"We're not going to Madrid, Luis. We're going north to Comillas. Your parents are there. It will be a long trip," Modesto answered.

I then leaned back in the car seat. I began to think about Sister Esther, Pablo, and the piano. There will be a piano there and I will get to play, right? But will I be able to see Sister Esther again?

The wheels of the car lulled me to sleep and time passed. Between my dreams I heard Sister Esther's voice, the piano out of tune, the water of the old mill, and the croaking of Astolfa and Rigoberta, the fountain toads. Modesto watched me through the mirror and his face gave me peace of mind.

4
The Interview

On October 11, 2006, I interviewed Mr. Luis Antonio Muñoz-Gómez for the last time. I arrived at his house in the Teusaquillo neighborhood around 3:45 that afternoon. I remember it was raining and cold. The meeting was supposed to be a day before, but Luis canceled it at the last moment. When Alicia called me and confirmed the meeting, I thought I might be facing my last chance to ask everything. And so it was. Months later, Luis died.

The week before, I had dinner with Jorge at Zona-G. We had the opportunity to discuss details of the project, especially a final interview. Jorge was determined that we would shoot the meeting with Luis, but I did not agree. Jorge had seen the material we had done in Agua de Dios and knew the story we had very well. The only thing missing, according to him, was a filmed interview with Luis himself. I knew that would be impossible. I also knew that any ill-advised move would damage the meeting.

That night I slept very little. There were many things that tormented me. I had become passionate about an unusual story that was slowly wearing me down. Sometimes, like Luis says, the past is like a knife that cuts through you, wounds you, and kills you. In this case, I was inserting that knife myself. With all that I had researched, my only question was, "Why all this interest on the part of an outsider in bringing this story to light?"

I sat, as usual, in the chair that was located in the hallway, right next to the stairs. Everything was silent. Even Bach was playing in complete silence. I decided to get up and head for the bathroom. I made myself a line and snorted it. It had been a long time since I had done that. The last time, Andrea had been very upset. I sat back down in the chair. I was calmer. After a while Alicia arrived. I don't know how much time had passed. It must have been after four o'clock. I don't know why the image of Andrea came back to me. Everything had become confused. While I was thinking, Alicia was talking to me; she only seemed to move her lips. She was wearing a light blue suit and the hem of her dress was in white crochet. She reminded me of my grandmother and my aunts, the ones they call "spinsters." Andrea came back to me. Alicia continued to move her lips. I think it was four past four. Again.

Alicia knocked on Luis's study door. She opened it slowly, with impeccable ceremoniousness. She walked in and adjusted it. Then she leaned out and invited me in.

"Would you like a drink?" she asked.

"As usual, a whiskey on the rocks," I said.

Luis was a slow man. He usually talked as much as he needed to and listened more. He loved music more than life itself. He said that without music life had no meaning. He listened to everything, he said, but the times we met he was always listening to Bach.

I was in the United States when I first heard about Luis's story. I had traveled to New York with the purpose of selling a script to a film production company (an ambitious project for me at the time) when a woman named Alicia called me. She told me over the phone that she was very interested in having me direct a project based on a book that Luis, her partner, had written. It sounded like a big project. She also told me that my last novel, *Carlota, la puta Ingenua*, had served as a reference for her. We agreed to talk to each other when I returned, but my stay in New York was extended, and it was not until many months later that I heard from her again.

LUIS TURNS ON a small lamp on his desk. The dim light allows me to see some photographs. One shows him and Alicia at a party, another shows his parents, and the last one shows a priest. We have been talking for four hours. He more than me…

Then, he continued:

Located forty-five minutes from Santander, in the province of Cantabria, Comillas was known as the town of the archbishops. Surrounded by mountains and sea, it ate and drank well. There was always a party, hustle and bustle, people in the streets singing and dancing…

Comillas brings back many memories, dear Leonardo, like that first love that you never forget. A beautiful town, where I spent summers and winters in the company of my parents, books, and music.

(Silence).

Next to the port the beach extends and, behind it, some buildings of the summery Comillas: The *Casa del Sagrado Corazón*, the cemetery, the park, and a beautiful building, called *Casa del Inglés*, which seems to be taken out of an illustration in a storybook. There I spent long hours gazing at the sea and its infinity. I also remember the cemetery, located on a small hill, among the ruins of an old church of the sixteenth century, with some modernist mausoleums and an elegant and imposing entrance.

A GENTLE HAND ran over my face. I opened my eyes and immediately recognized the motherly face of my new and, at the same time, only mother.

"Welcome home, Luis" said a breathy voice.

Her bright blue eyes, black hair and pale face made my heart rest in complete harmony. My father, just as lovingly, carried me in his arms to the main entrance of the house.

Everything was new to me. Only a child of that age could overcome with a certain indifference the radical changes I was experiencing. I showed gratitude and tranquility in those moments, but only my heart knew how much suffering I had experienced. A few hours before I was leaving a poor and abandoned orphanage, and now everything was opulence and festivity.

That night there was a party at home. At first I thought it was my homecoming, but then I realized it was part of everyday life in Comillas. I was sent to play with the other children there. I remember they were all very good to me—and in their innocence, they showed little interest in learning about my past. My parents' friends, on the other hand, and especially my mother's friends, always looked at me—at least in the early years, with a certain tenderness wrapped in compassion. I decided to do my best and conform without reproach. If this was what I had always dreamed of, why complain?

Comillas was the fashionable place to spend summers and winters. When vacations approached, the only thought was to organize the trip. Most of my new friends had homes there, so you felt like you were in Madrid, only with a good climate, enjoying the warm sun in the winters and fresh air in the summers.

Vacations began the same day we finished school. That Friday I would come home, I would change, and we would put all the luggage in the car. Modesto was in charge of getting the house ready for departure, with everything locked and double-checked. Hortensia took care of the market, the food, and the snacks for the road. My father prepared the boxes with wines, liquors, and champagne, and my mother took care of me.

After a few hours of travel, and before arriving in Comillas, my parents made a short stop in Ontaneda to visit the Bustamante family. It was part of the every year tradition. We would spend one or two nights there, depending of the parties.

(Silence).

Ontaneda was a very small town—too small to remember…

While we were there I liked to swim and go for walks. I never found a place like the old mill, however, which I always remembered when I hiked there—but I entertained myself and enjoyed what I could.

When it was almost noon and the sun was setting brightly, I would lie down under a tree. Then I would go back to the house and let the time pass.

When evening came, my parents would have endless dinners. I would go to sleep, looking forward to getting the hell out of there. The Bustamantes had their sons living in Mexico, so the house always felt empty and cold, even with us in it. At some point I thought my mother had been in love with Santiago Bustamante, the father—but it doesn't matter anymore.

As a child, life in Comillas was quiet. Then, as a teenager, I began to go out and enjoy the nightlife. We all grew up in it, watching it grow old.

I spent my last summers and winters before leaving with my childhood friends. I really enjoyed them to the fullest. I remember that we used to go hiking. We would walk around the lighthouse and the mountain and go to nearby places, such as Cóbreces. There I would visit my friend Juan, a monk who lived in the Viaceli Abbey, whom I had known since I first came to Comillas. We also would visit Rosa, in La Barquera, and Damian and Antonio in Novales. At night we would go to the beach. There we would make bonfires while Carmen played the guitar. After we'd take a bath, and then we would play like fools, smoking, drinking and dancing until we were dead.

During that last summer I was melancholic. I think I knew it would be my last one, at least in that way. I remember that on one of those days I accompanied my mother to the flea market to buy fruit and a new broom. We walked slowly and distantly down Duque de Longaz Street, which ended at the square. I noticed in the distance, next to the statue of Cervantes, a man selling used books. I approached him just out of curiosity. That was the first time I encountered Goethe's *Faust* and Dante's *Divine Comedy.* I already knew of the works and, in fact, we had them at home—but it was the first time I was interested in them. I bought both books, and in my room, sitting at the window, watching the square and the street around the house, I spent the whole summer reading them. An indelible memory that has never ceased to visit me.

As time went by, the fearful personality I had once had begun to fade. Now I was an intelligent, responsible boy, full of countless qualities that made my parents prouder and prouder every day.

When the vacations were over, we returned to Madrid, to our studies, to everyday life, to wait for winter and another trip to Comillas. It was a circle that revolved around a summer and a winter, around those hours that we never forget.

(Silence).

In Madrid, my life was divided between school, Sunday mass, music, and parties with friends. Piano lessons were never absent. I think Sister Esther would have been very proud to know that. My teacher, Irene, had been a concert pianist in her time and was a very good pedagogue. She would arrive in the afternoons full of books and sheet music for me to study. Then, on Fridays, my father would have a get-together and invite all his friends. On those evenings I would play everything I had learned. That's how I got over the fear of playing in public and learned to debate with passion. My language was sharpened by being around my parents' friends, who were intellectuals and liberal politicians.

I never heard from the orphanage again. I never heard from my classmates, the Mother Director, or Sister Esther. I continually asked my mother to write to them, to pay them a visit, but she always replied that the wisest thing to do was to leave that book closed and forget. Thus, I returned to the beginnings, to the oblivion, always present in my life.

As time went by, I forgot where I had come from. I professed my love for my parents on a daily basis, and of those times of pain and loneliness only a few lukewarm memories remained, which rarely appeared anymore. I quickly learned the rules of the game and chose to keep quiet and not ask questions. I knew that in the end I was not free, because we are not free.

(Silence).

My questions began to disappear. All the material I had prepared before the visit was now subsumed under a new story. It seemed as if I was only there to listen and not to ask questions. It would not be easy for me to go back to the beginning, I thought. Now I could only listen attentively to what Luis wanted to share with me. My work was becoming a maze full of stories, many of them insignificant to me. But there I was, like a sculpture, still and bored, listening attentively to the old man's story. The interview was prearranged and I could only listen and wait.

LUIS'S VOICE DISAPPEARS. The studio is quite and now we hear the chords of a guitar. Everyone is sitting on the floor. Catalina, Alfonso's girlfriend, is singing a bolero. There is a lot of liquor and everyone is drinking. Alfonso is a little drunk. Next to him is Alejandro, his best friend; next to Alejandro is Francisca, his girlfriend (They affectionately call her Pacha, or Pachita). Alfonso goes to the bathroom and beckons Alejandro to come with him. When they are both inside, Alfonso takes out a bag of coke. He sits on the toilet seat and begins to crack the coke. Alejandro takes out a five-thousand-peso bill, rolls it up and shoves a line through his left nostril. Then he does the same on the right side. He passes the bill to Alfonso while he wipes his shirt and looks at himself in the mirror.

"Am I all right?" Alfonso asks.

"Yes, and me?" asks Alejandro as he finishes his coke.

"Yes, you're fine."

"Did you hear? Cata sings fucking amazing, doesn't she?"

"Phew, impressive," Alfonso answers.

"Are you in love?" asks Alejandro while Alfonso puts the coke away.

"What a question! Of course, man!"

Alejandro stares at him. Alfonso notices by the reflection in the mirror.

"What's the matter?"

"Nothing, man. Wipe that off."

Alejandro brings his hand to Alfonso's nose and wipes his nose. Alfonso leaves the bathroom and goes to the terrace, where Catalina is.

"Can I have a cigarette?" asks Alfonso.

Catalina opens her purse and takes a pack of Marlboro Reds. Then she takes a lighter out of her pocket. As she lights Alfonso's cigarette, she asks him: "Could you change the itinerary?"

"No. The festival is scheduled for the day after I arrive, so I can't," Alfonso answers.
Catalina does not hide her displeasure.

"I swear that with these trips it's impossible to maintain a relationship. Now we hardly see each other anymore."

"Cata, stop," answers Alfonso.

"You don't have time anymore. And when you're not with Fernando, recording or traveling, you're with Alejandro partying."

"Cata, seriously, stop talking nonsense. It's not worth it. We're spending New Year's together in Cartagena with your family, aren't we? Relax."

Alfonso hugs Catalina and kisses her. Alejandro watches from the kitchen door.

The next day, Alfonso is startled awake. The sound of his phone on the nightstand has woken him up. Catalina is naked next to him. Alfonso looks at the phone and immediately jumps out of bed. He showers, dresses with the first thing he finds in a half-open suitcase, and leaves. A black van is waiting for him in front of the building entrance. Beatriz, his assistant, is standing outside the car with a coffee in her hand.

Alfonso greets Beatriz with a kiss and gets into the car. He wears black glasses and has a stench. Beatriz passes him the coffee, opens the window, and takes the newspaper out of her purse.

"Today there was an article in *El Tiempo* about the movie," says Beatriz.

"Oh, really? Let's see, read me a little bit yourself, I can't stand this hangover."

"Actor Alfonso Santamaría has arrived in the country to start shooting *El Castigo de Dios*, the new film by Gretel Ibáñez, which tells the story of Agua de Dios and its beginnings as a lazaretto. The artist, son of the assassinated representative to the Chamber of Deputies, Dr. Pedro Santamaría, was away from film for two years after being admitted to a detoxification clinic in New York following several scandals in the Big Apple. Santamaría is currently in one of the most successful periods of his career. He won the Goya Award for best actor for his role in *La investigación*, the latest film by Spanish Director Borja Fernandez. He is currently based in Los Angeles with his girlfriend, actress and singer Catalina Jaramillo, with whom he has been in a relationship for more than a year, following his controversial breakup with English actress Sophia Kramer. It is said that, for this movie, the artist…"

"Hand me your phone, please, so I can call Alejandro," Alfonso says to Beatriz, interrupting her reading.

"Just a second," Beatriz answers, as she quickly folds and puts away the newspaper.

"Hey, Alejo, how are you doing?"

(Telephone conversation)

"That's how I'm doing. I don't know how I'm going to roll. I'll have to have extra coffee and a Red Bull, otherwise…"

(Telephone conversation).

"A little bit. A little upset, but well, she will get over it. You know how women are."

(Telephone conversation)

"Yes, exactly. The usual. The trips, the studio, you know. I have no problem with that, but she's the one who came here to record that soap opera. It's her job, but I can't come here every two weeks. I told her that."

(Telephone conversation)

"Yes, Beatriz just read it. The usual. You know, the journalism here… Hey, why don't you stop by the rehearsal?"

(Telephone conversation)

"Okay, I understand. No problem, I'll still see you tonight at Andrés. We'll have a good one today." Alfonso ends the call and hands the phone to Beatriz, who continues reading the newspaper.

"Look, this is really interesting. There's a review in *El Espectador*," says Beatriz, while she reads the article with concentration.

"Let's see, read it," says Alfonso as he takes a sip of coffee.

"The shooting of *El Castigo de Dios*, the new film by Gretel Ibáñez and starring Alfonso Santamaría, Lina Cuesta, and Juan Sebastián Herrera, has begun at the Teatro Colón in Bogotá. The film narrates the love between a doctor who arrives in Agua de Dios for his rural year and a young leper who lives with the nuns. The story also narrates a piece of music, apparently belonging to Luis Antonio Calvo and composed in 1921, that was found in the house of the Maestro (which is today the Calvo Museum) by a group of researchers who were making a documentary about his life and work. *El Espectador* spoke exclusively with Mrs. Alicia Turbay, manager and co-producer of the film, who is said to have played a role in the discovery of the musical piece."

ALICIA IS SITTING in the garden of her house. It is the same house where she lived with Luis. In the background you can see the halls leading to what used to be his studio. She and the journalist are sitting at a table. There is a tape recorder in the center, documenting the interview.

"Alicia, please tell us how this project came about."

"Well, I am very happy to be part of this project, and above all to fulfill the promise I made to Luis, which is to make the documentary and the film."

"Tell us a little more about the musical work."

"Luis Antonio was always in love with Calvo's music, and it was through him that he got to know Agua de Dios. When Ana de Calvo died and left her house to the town, Luis began to manage, along with other people, the preservation of Maestro Calvo's legacy. By the year 2000, Luis already had the idea of making a documentary and a film, based on a book he was writing. However, this would not materialize until 2006, which is when we started working hand in hand with Leonardo Campos, the project's writer and scriptwriter."

"Is the documentary available yet?"

"No. It is not finished yet. We are waiting on some film images that we want to include in the documentary."

"Regarding the music page, some musicologists have doubted Calvo's authorship, because it is a work that bears no relation to his compositional aesthetics. What do you think?"

"I have already said many times that the work is not by Calvo. Yes, it is his handwritten and it was found in his house, but he is not the composer. Luis was a great scholar of Calvo's work. He concluded that this work was possibly by one of his students, which Calvo would have helped to write for some reason unknown to us. I know it may sound a bit strange, but, as Luis said, it is not at all impossible. These practices were common among teaching musicians of the time, especially when the student did not master musical writing. We also know that

Calvo had many students while he lived in Agua de Dios, so it would not be strange if this had happened."

"When was the piece written?" asks the journalist.

"We know it was written in 1921," answers Alicia. "At that time Calvo lived in Agua de Dios, and we know it was a very difficult time for him. People know very little about Agua de Dios—that it was a place for lepers and nothing else. But the truth is that Agua de Dios was a concentration camp, and I think the music represents that pain."

"You recently said that it was very moving that the shooting of the film began at the Teatro Colón. Why is that?"

"Yes. When Calvo was diagnosed with leprosy, Bogotá's society paid tribute to him at the Teatro Colón before he left for Agua de Dios. Almost a century later, *El Maestro* returns to the Colón. I feel that this is very moving."

"Is my dressing room ready?" Alfonso asks, interrupting Beatriz's reading.

"Yes, *La pulga* has already arrived and has everything ready. Fernando should be here soon.

"I need to get some sleep," says Alfonso, yawning.

"Shall I confirm the dinner with the Mexican people for after the shooting?"

"No, not at all. Don't go around making plans. We're organizing one of those little parties we like. Come if you want with Marcelo."

"Another one?" Beatriz asks sarcastically. "But if you have an interview right after with the magazine…"

"I don't feel like it. Change it for another day," Alfonso replies.

"But what other day?! You're going to LA!" The driver parks the car a block away from the Teatro Colón. Alfonso takes his jacket, gets out of the car, and throws the door open.

"WHY DID YOU think you were not free?" I asked.

"Freedom is a word I don't know yet," said Luis.

To know whether we are free or not, or, rather, whether we can be free or not, I think is the least we should ask ourselves as thinking individuals. But the truth is that we don't. To know whether what we have done since we can remember, or what we have planned to do as a life project, was or will be the product of the exercise of our freedom or the whim of a God, is simply terrifying.

"And what does it mean to you to be free?" I asked.

"A lot is said about freedom," Luis answered. Some think that man is not free at all, because all his activity is regulated by behavioral guidelines that tell him what he should and should not do. And to this is added the dilemma of what the individual decides or does not decide to do, giving another meaning to the word freedom: free will. But I am not a philosopher and I do not like to sit and think about issues that life itself teaches us over time. I am no longer anxious, dear friend. But I don't have the time either. Time is a gift that one day they give to you and the next day they take away. We seek the truth, even if it is unconsciously. And the study of truth is the very object of that desire. Juan said that there is my truth, your truth, and the truth. So, is truth subjective?"

(Silence).

Leonardo is thoughtful…

"According to Thomas Aquinas in his famous *Summa Theologiae*, truth is defined as 'the adequation of thing and intellect,'" Luis continues. "That is, first that which exists, and then that which is known by the human mind. However, history has encountered different ways of seeing or denominating truth. This is referred to in several books. Skepticism denies that human beings are capable of attaining the truth of things, and therefore postulates that it is impossible to know reality. On the other hand, relativism holds something similar, and is the most common today. Everything is true or false depending on the glass through which one looks at it. However, both fall under their own weight. If, as skepticism teaches, no proposition is true, then the statement that nothing is true is also false. And if no opinion is definitive and everything is equally true, as the relativists teach, then neither can we determine the validity of the statement of the one who proposes that everything is equally true. Thus, each of us is free to decide what best suits our circumstances or desires. There can be only one truth, even when we find different truths created by our egos."

"I see your point," I said. "And how long were you in Madrid?"

FERNANDO IS ORGANIZING some papers on the table in the dressing room when Alicia knocks on the door. Alfonso is leaning on a sofa.

"Alicia, what a surprise! I saw you a while ago at the rehearsal. What did you think?" Fernando says to her, as he closes the dressing room door.

"It was wonderful, Fernando. It was impossible not to fly with the music." Says Alicia while observes Alfonso leaning back on the sofa.

"I'd like to congratulate Alfonso," Continues Alicia.

"I don't think this is a good time," Replies Fernando. "He had an argument with his girlfriend this morning. He didn't sleep well and I don't think he's comfortable with the scene. Why don't we leave it for later?"

"I won't be long. I just want to talk to him about something before the next shooting," says Alicia. "I've tried several times to see him since he arrived to Colombia, but it's been impossible."

"I understand. Let me ask," answers Fernando.

Fernando approaches the sound equipment on the table. It is the same table where he was organizing the scripts. Alfonso is still lying on the sofa. He is looking at his phone. The dressing room is large.

There is a table with bottles of water, a bowl, fruits, magazines, and a newspaper. Electronic music is playing.

"Alfonso," Fernando whispers.

"What is it?" Alfonso answers, annoyed.

"I'm sorry. I don't want to bother you, but Alicia Turbay is here. She says she'd like to talk to you for a second. I've told her it's not a good time, but she insists. She says she's been trying to see you for days."

"Now? Why don't you tell her… ?"

Alicia interrupts the conversation:

"I'll be just a moment. I assure you I won't be long."

Alfonso gets up again, runs his hands through his hair and sits down on the sofa. Fernando motions for Alicia to sit down and then disappears without a word. Alfonso lights a cigarette. He approaches the sound system and turns up the volume.

"Alicia, I'm sorry we haven't been able to talk," Says Alfonso. "Beatriz told me that you called several times. It's just that there have been events and things and time flies by."

"Oh, It's okay, Alfonso," Says Alicia. "I understand."

"I saw you at the rehearsal. What did you think?" Alfonso asks curiously.

"I know we don't have much time, so I'll get to the point," Says Alicia. "The night Luis died, when he was dying, he gave me a folder with some letters. There were also photos and other things. Luis wrote in his diary everything he knew, what he had researched about Agua de Dios. He was very determined to make the documentary."

Alicia opens her purse and takes out a folder and a bag.

"Here I have the recordings of the meetings between Leonardo Campos, the writer of the documentary, and Luis. I think you should listen to them before continuing with the filming. In the folder you will find photocopies of some letters we found. I will also leave you the manuscript of Luis's book. I think it is important that you read it."

"Alicia, I'm flattered that you want to share these things with me," Says Alfonso.

"I'll see if I manage to read it, because time is the only thing I don't have at the moment."

"You will. You still don't understand what you are doing. Maybe it's time to let go of your ego and pretension. Maybe it's time to grow up and really be an artist rather than an actor for the moment. This is not about learning scripts and repeating them in front of the camera. This is about bringing a character to life, and the veracity of this story is up to you."

Agua de Dios, June 10, 1921

Dear Julio,

I can't take it anymore. The days without you are complete misery. Maestro came to visit me today. His pain saddens my days even more. Those days... the days without you. Those, the ones that are a complete misery.

(Silence).

Alfonso remains pensive at what he has just read. He is sitting on the sofa of his hotel. Alicia's words had hurt him. Who did that old woman think she was to talk to him like that?

"BY THE END OF 1940 the situation in Spain was becoming increasingly complicated and uncertain." Said Luis.

Franco held the reins of the party, the army, and the government. The civil war was ending, the dictatorship was beginning. My parents thought it would be wiser for me to leave Spain and take advantage of this time to study. It was time to learn other languages and get to know other cultures. So I went to Paris. During the time I was studying, my parents visited me quite often. Even in the following summers we saw each other in Comillas, although as time went by I was not as interested as I had been before.

In Paris I learned to see life with different eyes. I became obsessed with the arts and with artists. I met many: basic, good, bad, complex, happy, sad, but in the end, artists, as I intended to be. I became obsessed with philosophers, with composers and rebels. I began to question things I never questioned before: love, God, faith, religion, chance, and destiny. The words that man clings to when he is on the edge of the abyss. But the abyss was the answer, I thought. I got tired of being correct and saying what others expected me to say…

(Silence).

…In Paris I also understood that I would always be alone…

(Silence).

Luis stands in front of the window. It is still raining. All those days it rained. I listen attentively and take note:

By 1943 World War II ruled us. That year was especially hard for us. Having finished my studies in Criticism, I decided to return to Spain and spend some time with my parents, who were getting a bit older.

I took a job at a college as an assistant to a friend of my father's. I didn't earn much, but it kept me busy.
My parents, especially my father, became very angry. We would argue about everything. He started pressuring me to get married and run the family business. At that time, by my age, twenty-two, people already had a family, he said. But I didn't want to. I didn't go out much and I didn't go to parties with people my age. After Paris, people in Madrid seemed to me to be complete imbeciles. My mother seemed

to suffer more than I did from my father's reproaches. Madrid and its questions suffocated me. My parents also suffocated me. A few months later I returned to Paris.

5
The Return

When I came back from New York I continued working for the television channel. I had to make a living. I knew that film projects were slow and I couldn't just sit around waiting for the New York production companies to call me back.

The work at the channel was always the same. I knew that after a while I would be bored again and looking for other things. I had also decided not to write again, or at least not seriously. *Carlota, la puta ingenua* had not produced the results I had hoped for and I felt I was a failure as a writer.

After a few months, with no response from New York, I called Diana and asked her to help me look for other job opportunities. She had contacts and was sharing content and talent with several international production companies, especially in Mexico and Miami. It was then that I heard from Alicia again.

Diana told me that Alicia had been calling her office for days. She told me that she had told her about the project and explained that it had a very good budget. The only thing that Diana saw as complicated at that moment was that Alicia demanded that I dedicate myself exclusively to the project. This was her only condition. I would have to research, travel, do interviews, and prepare and produce a documentary based on the stories. I would also have to look for talent. Diana told her that she thought it would be very difficult for me to commit myself exclusively.

Still, seeing the situation I was in, Diana suggested that I call Alicia and hear what the project was about. There weren't many opportunities at the time, and the money Alicia was offering was ridiculously tempting. It wouldn't hurt to have a meeting with her and hear her out. So I decided to contact her that same day.

We met the following week at a café. Alicia brought a folder with some papers, asked me to read it, and told me that when I finished it we would talk again.
That same night I began to read it:

I RETURNED TO SPAIN after seven years. It was 1951.

Although during those years I traveled to Madrid at Christmas, my parents no longer wanted me to be so far away. That would be my last Paris-Madrid trip. I was thirty years old.

Things at home were not going well. My parents were getting older and needed my attention. Business was not going well either. I had grown up. I had studied Architecture and Criticism. I also had a Master's degree in Business, spoke three languages, and loved to travel. I was no longer afraid of myself or my parents. I then decided to put aside my things, including criticism and music, and focus on my father's business.

For the next three years, my life was quiet. I dedicated myself to learning everything I needed to know about the family business. I knew that soon my father would be gone, and then I would have to take care of everything. In my personal life, everything remained the same. I was still that lonely and sad man who thought only about his past and who still woke up at night overwhelmed by dreams.

One night, after coming home from the office, I sat down at the piano and began to play. It was the first time I had done so for a long time. I immediately went back to Salamanca, to the orphanage, and then I saw Sister Esther's face. I closed the lid of the keyboard, furious, and went to my room. I threw myself on the bed. My head was spinning. What had happened to all of them? Why did I never go back? How many years had passed without even allowing myself to look back at my childhood memories! I felt dejected and ungrateful. It was as if the orphanage had meant nothing to me. How could I live in peace, if all I did in my life was avoid the questions?

That night I stayed awake. At five o'clock in the morning, when the day was already dawning, I went for a run to clear my mind. While I was running I thought a lot. I thought about the orphanage, the Sisters, Pablo, the music. I was curious and I felt the need to know what had happened to everyone. I also thought it was strange that this feeling had awakened again, just now, and that maybe I should follow my intuition. I hadn't done anything wrong either. We have the right to forget the past, and maybe we also have the right to forget the mistakes. I guess I wasn't happy and maybe I didn't have the time to realize that anymore. Maybe that's why I was looking for answers in the past, as if the orphanage was going to give them to me, I thought. It was possible that I was just looking to learn more about myself. I had a right to that, too, I thought.

After an hour I sat down on the park bench and decided to return to Salamanca. I had no excuse not to. The very idea reassured me. I felt it was going home, back to that home that I still was mine. I returned home and talked to my parents. I told them I was going hunting with friends for the weekend. After breakfast I went to work and started to get everything ready for the trip.

MAESTRO CALVO CLOSES the door. Esteban looks haggard and tired. With difficulty, he gets out of bed and begins to write. It is a large space. In front of his desk is a window:

> *...Today has been a hot day. This morning sister Josefina visited me. She brought me fruit from the orchard. She told me that Mr. Jorge feels the same and that he asks a lot about you. She also told me that there is a new doctor who is taking care of the new patients. I am waiting to feel better so I can meet him...*

6
Julio

It was dark when we arrived in Tocaima. I had secured a cottage through a friend of Ana's that was located only fifteen minutes from Agua de Dios. It was the perfect place to start pre-production. We traveled with a group that included a photographer, an assistant, and three cameramen that I brought with me from the tv-channel. Diana and a couple friends of hers were also on the trip. I was very interested in getting her involved in the project, and she was Ana's friend. The music accompanied me during the whole process, as Luis had requested.

By then, I had already gathered a lot of information from my previous visits. I had interviewed relatives of leprosy patients and watched a couple of short documentaries about Agua de Dios. I had also read Dr. Abel Fernando Martinez's research: *Church, State and Leprosy in Colombia*. On the other hand, I had the information Luis had given me. It was clear to me that Agua de Dios was not what people knew—a simple place where leprosy patients were confined—but that it had also functioned as a prison for political opponents. A place of experimentation on the sick, where ethics and dignity did not exist and where the most atrocious and inhuman acts that one can imagine were practiced. It was no coincidence that it was called the city of pain.

We left Bogotá on Thursday afternoon. The plan was to work all day Friday and Saturday and rest on Sunday, taking advantage of the holiday weekend. On Monday, after lunch, we would return to Bogotá.

We got organized in the rooms and then gathered by the pool. We opened beers and wine and the home's cook prepared some tapas for us. I went back to talk to the team about the plan for those two days and what I was looking to document.

After the meeting, the owner of the house invited us to lie down on the grass next to the pool and watch the sky. He turned off all the lights in the estate and played excerpts from *Madama Butterfly*. I lit a joint while I looked at the sky. The Tocaima sky was starry that night and with the lights off in the house it shone beautifully.

The next day we left very early for Agua de Dios. This was my fifth visit. During the drives I tried to imagine what that same trip would have been like a hundred years ago: the horses, the severe sun, the difficult road, the embarrassment of the patients, the pain… Whenever I was there, I thought the same thing.

Our first stop: *El Puente de los Suspiros* (Bridge of Sighs).

Built in 1862, the bridge was baptized with the same name as the bridge that, in Venice, connects the Doge's Palace with the former prison of the Inquisition, crossing the Di Palazzo River. It owes its name to the sighs of the prisoners who, from there, saw the sky and the sea for the last time. In Colombia, the Bridge of Sighs, the first suspension bridge in the country, crosses over the Bogotá River and connects Tocaima with Agua de Dios. This was the last place where patients said goodbye to their families before isolating themselves forever from the world. For many it also meant a bridge separating good from evil, life from death, sadness from joy.

We arrived at the mayor's office. I went to the cultural office and asked for the person in charge of the Calvo Museum (Days before I had contacted him to coordinate the visit). I remember that it was very hot and there were many flies in the main square. We started filming immediately at the Calvo Museum. For that first meeting we invited journalists and people who had settled in the area, not because they had leprosy, but because they were accompanying a sick family member. The person in charge of the museum started the meeting by welcoming us.

By that fifth visit, I had already completed most of the research work and was almost ready to start shooting. However, I still did not know the other story that Luis did not tell. The story that he did not share in our first meetings and that he left solely for our last meeting. Maybe it was because he didn't want there to be time for questions, I thought.

"I REMEMBERED almost nothing of Salamanca," Continues Luis. Only the old mill, Sister Esther's piano, Pablo, and the Tormes River came to my mind. I didn't know where I would sleep, but I didn't care. The only thing I wanted was to get to the orphanage.

I arrived in the afternoon. The beauty of the Salamanca landscape was still intact. The orphanage was the same, only with a fresh paint job. I passed by the fountain, which was also still the same, with its toads; I don't know if they were Astolfa and Rigoberta, but they were very similar. In the background, the dome, and next to it, the entrance.

I knocked on the door several times. A man in his sixties greeted me.

"Good afternoon," I said. "I am looking for the Mother Director, Teresa de Jesús."

"I don't know any sister by that name," the man declared. "Is this the place you are looking for?"

"Is this the San Ignacio orphanage?"

"Yes, it is," he confirmed, "but I told you there is no sister by that name."

"Could you take me to the person in charge of the center? I come from Madrid and I don't have much time."

The doorman had me follow him and told me to wait in the hallway of the Mother Director's office. My heart was pounding as I silently walked. I had not forgotten the way. The room had new, black furniture. I sat impatiently, waiting for the nun to greet me.

At last I entered the office. It was the same as before. The nun invited me to sit in the small room next to her desk.

"What can I do for you?" she asked.

"You see, sister. I lived here for the first years of my life. I think about ten years. I understand that I was only months old when I arrived. Now, for personal reasons, I would like to have the history of my adoption. I live in Madrid."

The nun did not have any problem giving me the information. I never knew if it was because of the financial help I provided to the orphanage, or because life had arranged it that way, but I was surprised that the nun had no major issues with the favor I was asking her.

The woman got up from her chair, put on a coat over it, and took a piece of paper out of her desk drawer. She handed it to me and asked me to write down the dates I had lived at the orphanage and my real name, if I had changed it. She also told me that many children passed through there and that it was often difficult to find the histories of the children.

Minutes became hours and hours became days. I looked closely at that image of St. Ignatius that had always frightened me. It no longer had that effect on me. Now, years later, I looked at it with affection. The desk was the same. I thought about how life was sometimes summed up in a second. I imagined that all those years had not passed. There I was, again, in a place I thought I would never return to. The smell hadn't changed; surely the experience hadn't either. Probably now, inside those walls, there was also a child waiting with hope for news. I began to sweat. I listened to the Director's footsteps. They reminded me of Mother Teresa's footsteps. "What would I find? Would it prove wise for me to go back to the past?" I wondered.

Memories came to life. Sitting in that same armchair, in front of the same fireplace, I felt as if time had never passed. Who would have thought that after so many years I would return to that place to ask about the past? My heart felt what it felt years ago. It was as if the same ghosts had returned to answer my questions.

The woman handed me a folder. I opened it without her noticing how nervous I was. I began to read. My tears were fighting to come out. My inner peace collapsed. Everything was now more uncertain and confusing. My imagination took me into unknown territories. I closed the folder and handed it to her. Then I asked about everyone who had lived with me during that time. Sara (that was the nun's name) answered that, over so many years, everything had changed a lot. The Mother Director had been transferred shortly after I had left the orphanage. Pablo had been adopted by an American couple, and other classmates had grown up and moved to other cities. She also told me that Sister Esther had died four years earlier from a fall while cleaning the only saint that adorned the small chapel.

I said goodbye to the kind woman and walked back down the halls. I walked down the stairs and headed for the main entrance. I said goodbye to the doorman and walked out. I got into the car, put my hands on my face and wept bitterly. Why was it all going back to the beginning, back to the source of my regrets, my anguish, my past?

The information in the adoption file was different than what I had been told. It was not even related to the stories I had always heard from the Mother Director and Sister Esther. "How could Sister Esther lie to me?" I thought. There were no Portuguese farmers. My parents' visit was not a coincidence, and my adoption had been arranged. The only truth in the story I had been told was that I had arrived at the orphanage at night.

According to the file, I arrived in the company of a Salesian priest named Julio García. The priest had been sent by the Directors of the congregation in Madrid to take an almost five-year-old boy named Luis to live at the San Ignacio orphanage, located in the province of Salamanca. The priest would be in charge of finding a family that could adopt little Luis. In the meantime, the orphanage would see to his education and upkeep. The matter was treated with the utmost confidentiality, and the Mother Director was ordered never to speak about it. "What could I possibly have to do with that congregation?" I thought to myself.

I decided not to stay in Salamanca that night. Although I was devastated, full of sadness and anger, I set out to return to Madrid. I felt disappointed again, not only with life, but with those around me; I felt that everything in the end was a lie and that I would have no peace if I did not know the truth. My biological parents needed to understand that I would not judge them and that it was my right to know who they were. I set out to find the priest who took me to the orphanage. I set out to get to the truth. Now more than ever it was clear to me.

I got home very late. I was exhausted. I had dinner and told my parents that I had come back early because I was not feeling well. My job now was to locate the priest's whereabouts. At the orphanage they didn't know where he lived, and asking more seemed unwise, especially in the condition I was in. I locked myself in my room and tried to sleep. The next day I would go to the Salesians' home. I needed an explanation.

(Silence).

Luis remains thoughtful for a moment. Then, looking fixedly at Leonardo, he says:

"There are things that would be better left forgotten. There are questions that are better not to ask. Was I ready to face the time? I wasn't. And now that I'm eighty-five, I'm not either."

(Silence).

LEONARDO CLOSED the folder thinking of about Agua de Dios. How many times had I passed by there? And I had never thought about what was happening there? I think all Colombians knew that lepers had lived there, but beyond that, I think no one knew their real story. I even vaguely remember my father once mentioned that a tax called the "lazaretto tax" had to be paid.

The next day I called Alicia. I had finished reading that night all the material she had given me at the café. I told her that I was very interested in Agua de

Dios and that I thought there was a great story to tell. I also told her that I was ready to fulfill the agreement and to meet Luis Antonio and interview him.

“FINDING THE whereabouts of the Salesian priest would not be an easy task,” Says Luis. Finding a priest in the Madrid of that time seemed almost impossible. Some were still in hiding because of the war and persecution. Dorota would be my support. My father’s secretary and a deeply devout Catholic, she knew the priestly life of the city very well. I was sure that with her help I would know where to start. The first thing would be to get to know the Salesian centers in Madrid. Then I would have to knock door to door until I found Father Julio García.

I got up at about half past eight in the morning. My anxiety overcame the sleeplessness of the previous night. I headed naked to the bathroom; I turned on the shower and let the tub fill up. Then I climbed in and sat down. I started touching myself. I was aroused. I tried to get my thoughts straight, but I couldn’t do it. I rested for a while until it was time.

I got dressed and had breakfast. As usual, my father was in the living room reading the newspaper and my mother was embroidering. It was the first time I saw them with resentment and distance. That couple, whom I called parents, and who had given me so much love, now filled me with anger and disappointment. I was sure they had to know the truth. "Why had they kept it from me, then?" I thought. I said goodbye and left the house. It was too late for complaints.

I arrived at Dorota's house. Her granddaughter told me she was at mass, so I waited. Thoughts came back to me. There was the orphanage again. Even now the ghosts that haunted me on winter nights were present. I couldn't get Sister Esther's face out of my mind either.

After half an hour, Dorota arrived. She was surprised to see me. I told her I was looking for a Salesian priest and that I knew she could help me. I only knew a couple of churches. I knew that with her my search would be quicker. Dorota seemed curious about my questions, but never said or asked anything. I think it was obvious that I didn't want to give more details.

Dorota suggested that I go first to *El Colegio de María Auxiliadora*, the main school for the Salesians and also known as *Salesianos Estrecho*. This school was very controversial during the civil war. In the minds of those on the left, especially, it used teaching as a cover to lure young people from the neighborhood. For others, it was simply full of mentally ill priests (There were even rumors of atrocities attributed to the priests, such as offering poisoned sweets to children). During that time of controversy, clericalists were often harassed by the masses. When the war began, the priests and their supporters fled and the militias entered the school, calling themselves the Fifth Regiment.

When I arrived, I first entered the chapel at the entrance of the school. They were at mass. I waited, then, like a repentant sinner awaiting absolution. Although I no longer believed in anything, I sat in one of the pews and prayed. When mass was over, I went to the entrance of the school.

The brother doorman there received me very kindly:

"What can I do for you?" He asked.

"I am looking for Father Julio García. Someone told me he lived here," I answered, hoping my lie would work.

"Yes, Father Julio lives here," he confirmed,

"But he is no longer receiving visitors. He is

very ill. Do you have a meeting with him? That would be weird," he added.

"No, I don't. I'm here on my mother's behalf. She has been a friend of his for a long time. She asked me to give him a donation for the congregation."

The brother doorman told me to wait in the foyer. I knew that when I told him about the donation, I would get what I wanted (like in Salamanca). I waited patiently and calmly. I felt that this time I was in the right place. I didn't have any expectations. I just wanted some peace. That was all.

The hours passed. The hours that do not forget…

(Silence).

More than fifty years have passed since that afternoon, dear Leonardo.

(Silence).

I go back to the beginning of this conversation: We all have a past and that past also has a past. We all have our stories, and the stories, sooner or later, are told. I am eighty-five years old. I have never married.

I live in the company of Alicia, my nurse, friend and confidant. I have a cat I call Bach, a watch that reminds me of the end, a drawing that brightens my days, music that has never forgotten me and, especially, I have *God's punishment*."

7
Agua de Dios

On Monday, after lunch, we returned to Bogotá. The whole team had been impressed with the stories of Agua de Dios. During our visit we had toured what had been the shelters, the hospital, and the market area. We also visited the thermal waters, where people often bathed to find relief. I had enough material to start a rough draft. In addition, I had the interviews, documentation, and historical support. It was time to put it all down on paper.

"But where to start? There were so many stories… I had to go to the very core of my story," I thought.

The first thing to do was to talk about Agua de Dios, because not even we Colombians know the history of it. For this, I will use excerpts from the writing *How Colombia managed to be the first leprosy power in the world: 1869-1916* by Abel Fernando Martínez, M.D. who explains very well, part of the situation in Agua de Dios and Colombia at that times.

Agua de Dios, or the city of pain, as it was known, is about three hours from Bogotá. Anyone would think that it is just another resort town, surrounded by extravagant mansions and luxurious cars, the same as

Tocaima and Girardot, two of Bogotá's favorite vacation towns, which are located next to Agua de Dios. However, its history is different. Agua de Dios is a forgotten town. Until 1963 it was the place where leprosy patients were isolated, a sad and desolate place that even today some people are afraid to enter.

The story goes that the town was born when a group of leprosy patients, banished from the neighboring town of Tocaima, were forced to invade a hacienda called *Agua de Dios* and build their homes there. Leprosy was gaining strength since the late 1880s. Many sick people were moving to Girardot and its surroundings to find comfort in the clime there and fight against this rare and obscure disease. The Church maintained the legend that leprosy was a divine punishment, and that those who had it were paying for the guilt of one of their ancestors. These stories, added to the scarcity of scientific information about the disease, produced chaos and fear. Poor, persecuted, and abandoned, leprosy patients had nowhere to go. For this reason, in 1867, the Colombian state bought the land from its owner, Mr. Manuel Murillo Toro, and used it as a lazaretto. Three years later, in 1870, Agua de Dios officially founded.

In 1886, Joaquín Vélez, Colombian minister to the Holy See, asked the Salesians for help. He wrote a petition directly to their founder, Father John Bosco: *"My government, the prelates and all those interested in the poor, are anxious to make the Colombian people share in the benefits that you provide to modern society."*

The following year, the archbishop of Bogotá, Monsignor José Telésforo Paúl, wrote to Don Bosco in the same vein. But the replies from Father Bosco respectfully explained the impossibility due to lack of personnel. The Colombian government then turned to Pope Leo XIII. The pontiff asked Cardinal Mariano Rampolla to write to Father Miguel Rúa, superior of the Salesians, to communicate his desire to accept the government's request so that the Salesians could found a mission in Colombia. The answer was affirmative. On January 10, 1890, under the orders of Father Miguel Unia, the first seven Salesians left for Colombia. Father Evasio Rabagliati, who had been appointed Director, was already on his way from Chile.

By September, the Salesians had already founded their first school in Bogotá, the *Colegio Salesiano de Leon XIII*. A year later, Father Miguel Unia began his apostolate in Agua de Dios. Upon arriving at the lazaretto, Father Unia wrote to his superiors recounting his experience: *"In Bogotá, which is so far from these unfortunates, when speaking of leprosy, Ave Maria! They are frightened, tremble with fear and do not even want to hear it mentioned."*

By the year 1891, the Church was already present in Agua de Dios with two congregations: the Salesians of Don Bosco and the Dominican Sisters of the Presentation. Both congregations would support the physical and mental health of the patients who arrived daily. Later, Father Luis Variara, who had arrived in the group of seven, would feel the need to create a new community, the Daughters of the Sacred Hearts of Jesus and Mary (HH.SS.CC.). This congregation would accept the vocations of infected patients, unlike the other two, which did not receive any novice who was a carrier of the disease.

In 1895, after the death of Father Miguel Unia, Father Evasio Rabagliati would be in charge of leading the leper issue and would be appointed chaplain of the country's lazarettos. Later, he would be called the "Apostle of the lepers."

After the civil war of 1895, Father Rabagliati gave a lecture on the great national lazaretto that was printed and distributed throughout the country. The Archbishop of Bogotá, in the name of the church and the homeland, highly recommended the work. Vice President Miguel Antonio Caro approved Father Rabagliati's initiative and asked the authorities for their support to *"Lay the foundations of a national lazaretto, as urgently demanded by the alarming spread of leprosy in several regions of the territory."*

On July 21, 1895, in response to an invitation from General Reyes, Rabagliati and Juan Manuel Restrepo met with twenty-one other people at Reyes's house. Among them were the presbyter Leopoldo Medina, Carlos Cuervo Márquez, Carlos Calderón, former minister of the Treasury, Bernardino Medina Calderón, a doctor from Boyacá, and Leo S. Kopp, a German industrialist. General Reyes presided over the meeting.

They convened for the purpose of deciding if in Colombia there was enough charity, patriotism, and instinct for self-preservation to save the nation from the terrible evil that threatened it: the prospect *"That our homeland becomes an immense lazaretto."*

General Reyes affirmed that, according to the latest statistics, there were 27,250 lepers in Colombia, a higher number than in the rest of America and

Europe. He invited the attendees to form a board, in association with Rabagliati, *"with the determined and enthusiastic collaboration of the clergy and charitable societies,"* in order to raise funds for the foundation of a great national leper colony.

In 1900, Vice President José Manuel Marroquín took power after a *coup d'état* against President Manuel Antonio San Clemente. Colombia was in the midst of the Thousand Days' War, with the divisions between the conservative and liberal parties threatening to destroy the country. In the aftermath of the civil war, the United States took advantage of Colombia's ungovernability to impose a treaty that granted it privileges over Panamanian territory. The objective was to build an interoceanic canal. The Hay-Herran-Hay Treaty granted the United States a five-kilometer strip on both sides of the canal and control over the maritime coasts. The government of Marroquín supported the treaty, but the Congress of the Republic rejected it. This unleashed the fury of the American government, which decided to support Panamá in its aspirations of independence from Colombia. On November 3, 1903, the United States proclaimed the independence of the Isthmus of Panamá, by means of a letter of notification to the Colombian Chancellery. Likewise, it placed warships in Panamanian territory in order to avoid a military response from Colombia. President Marroquín famously said: *"So what more do you want? They give me one republic and I give them two."*

The separation from Panamá, along with the consequences of civil war, left the country bankrupt. Leprosy began to spread rapidly, and the growing number of sick people shocked the country. In 1901, the entire city of Agua de Dios was cordoned off with a barbed wire fence and was guarded by the National and Internal Police, made up of leprosy patients themselves. Agua de Dios became an independent city with its own laws, its own currency (the coscoja), and a prohibition of intoxicating drinks. The Colombian government provided for the construction of a clinic, some hospitals, and a treatment subsidy called *la ración* (the portion).

In 1904, Rafael Reyes, who had just been elected president of Colombia, stated that leprosy was a more important problem for the country than railroads or public education. In his mind, it was a drama that had to be solved soon, otherwise Colombia would become *"...an immense leprosarium from which humanity would flee."* He added: *"This matter is more important to my country than paper money, than railroads, public instruction, than anything else. It is only comparable in its importance to the preservation of peace."*

In September of that same year, President Reyes sent to Congress an urgent circular with the purpose of *"extirpating leprosy"* by means of isolating the sick people: *"The time has come for the Legislative Branch, the Executive Branch and the entire nation to unite in order to undertake the national work of extirpating leprosy by isolating the sick in lazarettos."*

The president informed the congressmen of the opinion of Dr. Sauton, a French doctor and leprosy expert, on the exaggeration in the number of lepers: *"Although the disease has taken alarming proportions in our country, it is not greater than in other tropical nations, according to the study made in the state of Cauca by Dr. Sauton."*

In this way, the president corrected the opinion of those who claimed that Colombia was the country most attacked by leprosy.

Still, in 1905, under government decree, leprosy patients lost their civil rights and were placed in total and mandatory isolation. The lazaretto of Agua de Dios strengthened its wire fence. The rule ordered that each barbed strip had to be ten centimeters above the previous one, and two parallel fences had to be erected to prevent any contact with outsiders. Checkpoints were set up at all strategic points in Agua de Dios, with police surveillance, which prevented the sick from leaving and ensured their control. Depending on the areas of the country, patients could be sent to the lazarettos of Contratación, in Santander; Agua de Dios, in Cundinamarca; or Caño de Loro, Tierra Bomba Island. The latter had been in operation since the seventeenth century and housed the first lepers who arrived as slaves from Africa.

In the following year, 1906, the first official attempt to make a bacteriological diagnosis of leprosy was observed in the country. Pablo García Medina, assistant physician of the lazarettos section of the Ministry of Government, sent a circular to the governors, accompanied by capillary tubes and glass slides for physicians to send samples of lymph and nasal mucus of people suspected of leprosy. The objective in this case was to make a microscopic diagnosis of the disease in the central laboratory of lazarettos, created that year in Bogotá.

How many diseases were wrongly diagnosed as leprosy, according to Dr. Sauton, because of the lack of an accurate bacteriological diagnosis at that time? The differential diagnosis of leprosy today includes everything from scars to various diseases such as atopic dermatitis, erythema nodosum, scleroma, granulomas, leishmaniasis, lymphomas, lupus, morphea, neurofibromatosis, nevus, pityriasis, sarcoidosis, peripheral nerve tumors, and vitiligo.

In response to Garcia Medina's circular, Dr. Miguel Canales replied that leprosy is a disease *"of misery,"* that it is more frequent in the peasants and that *"the movement of people"* caused by the civil wars increased the number of affected people. *"Some sixty-five thousand lepers inhabit the Tenza Valley and not the thousand that were claimed two years ago, when the Boyacá lazaretto was to be built there."*

At the end of 1906, Dr. Julio Manrique Convers presented a report to the Ministry of Government, as special commissioner to Norway, to study the organization of leprosy hospitals. Julio Manrique regretted the lack of official leprosy statistics in Colombia and warned about the problems caused by the exaggeration of the number of lepers: *"The country is suffering real and true problems caused by the exaggerated data, provided by uneducated people in the matter, and which are daily published in foreign books and newspapers. In the maps that indicate the distribution of leprosy in the world and that appear in all the classic works, our country is stained with red, a color chosen to mark the abundance of the disease."*

Dr. Manrique adds that *"neither in India, which has thousands of lepers, nor in the Sandwich Islands or Hawaii, is the stigmatizing stain as large or as brightly colored as the one that marks our country."*

The news of such an alarming leprosy situation in Colombia was worrying for the authorities of an agro-exporting country. The exaggerated number of lepers in Colombia and the possibility that the products exported by the country were contaminated with the bacillus: *"...begins to cause panic in the European markets regarding our fruits, looking with suspicion at what comes from Colombia."*

Colombian exporters and authorities feared that European and North American markets would close to Colombian products for fear of leprosy contagion. The name "Colombian" was already synonymous with the word "elephantiac." Dr. Montoya y Flores, in 1906, without official statistics, already calculated an overall figure of only *"four to six thousand elephantiacs in the whole nation."*

The exaggeration of lepers in Colombia reached the incredible figure of *"more than 60,000"* in a country of five million inhabitants. The appearance of that number in a New York newspaper on August 4, 1906, generated a strong reaction from President Reyes. Concerned about the effect caused by the unstoppable exaggerations in the number of lepers, which Reyes attributed to Father Evasio Rabagliati, the president sent a circular letter to all the ambassadors and consuls of Colombia. Enclosed was a copy of the correction made by Dr. Julio Manrique, chief physician of the lazarettos of Colombia, to the assertion made by New York newspaper that there are more than sixty thousand elephantiacs in Colombia. The president urged that this correction be published in the local newspapers.

At the same time, he urged the consul in New York to send a note to the newspaper's management with Dr. Manrique's correction, demanding that it be published. If necessary, the newspaper would be paid for the insertion of the correction.

President Reyes asked the Colombian ambassadors and consuls to publish the correction in as many newspapers as possible: *"Send to the president the reproductions to make a pamphlet of them and circulate it abundantly, in order to correct by this means the error that has been made in affirming that Colombia is the country in the world where there are more lepers, something that has caused us immense problems and that could stop the immigration of the country."*

The sale of the Panama Canal, the conservative opposition to the government and the lack of knowledge and information regarding leprosy and its spread, threatened General Reyes's mandate to govern. The leprosy patients lost their possessions and their civil rights, and were confined, many of them against their will. The police raided villages, forcibly entered houses, and took people away. These acts began to generate violence within the community, and the sick began to live in what many would later be called concentration camps.

Adolfo León Gómez, a famous politician and writer whose liberal ideas got him sent to prison several times, presented in his book *The City of Pain: Echoes of the Prison of Innocents* evidence of the mistreatment and political persecution that took place in Agua de Dios.

According to Luis Fernando García Núñez, in his article "Anecdotes and Dramas: The Sufferings of Adolfo León Gómez (2013), Adolfo León did not received an examination during his twenty months in Agua de Dios, nor was he assigned a life regimen, much less given any legitimate treatment. Adolfo León himself writes that when he arrived at Agua de Dios, his name was now in *"the list of sick people, in the list of prisoners, in the list of beggars to whom, instead of individual and social rights, future and all, the loving fatherland gives thirty cents a day, sometimes reduced to half by the change of the repugnant special currency, so that they can pay for food, clothing, medicines, laundry, water and electricity services, servants, unavoidable alms, countless extraordinary expenses, etc. I was, therefore, enrolled and shod with the burning and indelible iron of the leprosarium."* And then, he had to *"serve as a laboratory rabbit for a few days, because, with immense hype and preceded by unprecedented fame, another infallible treatment was announced: gynocordate. Everyone awaited redemption with the same lively faith with which years before, according to the story, the lazaretto had awaited the treatment, also infallible, of the charlatan Angel Garcia, who, with another industrious gentleman, made a fortune from there and cured no one. If only he had cured someone, if not of the disease, at least of the mania of believing in exploiters of infallible remedies!"*

And about the treatment at Hospital Carrasquilla, he writes that it *"was a disaster. In a dirty and dismantled room, the only non-empty room in that abandoned and dilapidated building that cost the republic a great deal of money, a multitude of patients paraded one after another, some aggravated, others in good condition, old people, children, of all classes and categories (since many had received medication by direct order and personal payment), before the sick practitioner who, with not a few punctures, was successively giving them the injection, before the doctor who, at a prudent distance, did nothing but watch. From arm to arm, with the same bandage and the same needle already broken and bloody, without examination, without study, without considering the different conditions and circumstances of the patients, the gynocordate was introduced into the veins, which soon got obstructed. Nothing could be more unscientific, more repugnant, more rudimentary. Moreover, according to a written report sent by Dr. Montaña to Mr. Evaristo Quijano, it turned out that the powder dissolved in an unknown way introduced into our veins, had to be taken orally, in the absence of the tablets that the treatment prescribed. So, whoever did not have the disease there was given it from other patients, and whoever had it would easily catch another infection on top of it."*

The patients who arrived at Agua de Dios ended up wanting to conceal their presence there and hide under the cloak of oblivion, although the news spread quickly from mouth to mouth. In the same book, Adolfo León refers to this: *"Although I had to understand that the case was an 'open secret,' not only because of what the press had spread, but also because of what doctors who had not seen me even remotely said, and even more because of the viper whispers with which the human tongue spreads, with lightning speed, but always recommending inviolable secrecy. How much it harms others and how much it satisfies the malevolent and cruel curiosity with sensations and scandal."*

Adolfo León was assured on many occasions that no one in life had arrived in that sick city with more horror, more fear, more disgust, more compassion, and more sadness than him.

8
Esteban

Alicia enters the study and brings me ice, for the whiskey. Then she calls the cat, tenderly.

I continue to listen attentively to the old man's stories:

"Esteban arrived to Agua de Dios on March 1, 1909. He was then twenty-two years old. He had left against the wishes of his father and Carolina, his fiancée, with whom he had plans to marry that same year," says Luis.

The stories you heard about Agua de Dios were terrible. People said that everyone who lived there was crazy. They claimed that at night they only heard crying and moaning. They said that in the streets you would find pieces of bodies, fingers, arms, hands. They also said that, at night, they practiced diabolical rituals and homosexual orgies, and that whoever entered the place would never come out again.

In the hospital it seemed to be taboo to talk about what was going on there. The doctors didn't have much information, other than what the government provided through primers and advertisements. It seemed to be a mixture of terror, humiliation, and fiction. No doctor wanted to go. But Esteban was willing.

At first, I think Esteban was just looking for prestige, wisdom, and a lot of experience, perhaps. When you are twenty-two years old, you have a lot of ambitions and dreams.

(Silence).

I still dream, but I no longer have any ambitions…

Esteban was also looking for an identity, but he wasn't aware of that at the time. Agua de Dios became his trench. His life in the capital was unbearable. He had to flee at any cost, although he wasn't aware of that at the time.

Esteban studied medicine because it was what his father dreamed of. He never met his mother, so his father's love was all he had; he would never have contradicted his father's plans. He wanted to go to Europe and study in another country. Two of his good friends had left a few months earlier and were raving about what they were experiencing. Esteban, on the other hand, stared at his room. He thought of his father, drunk at night. He thought about that cold and empty society that tells you what to do, as if they had the morals to do it. He thought about Carolina and her desire to get married soon to please her mother, and about those endless dinners that bored him. It was depressing for him to read the letters from his friends, in which they told him about the freedom they were experiencing.

When Esteban finished his studies, he returned to the idea of going to Europe—this time, under the excuse of doing a specialization. But his father once again refused. A deep hatred began to grow slowly in his heart. He tried to hide it, but he knew it was there and that someday it would be too late to turn back.

Then it happened...

One of those nights, the government held a gala ball at the Teatro Colón. The purpose was to raise funds for the lazarettos and to explain in the voice of the person in charge of the apostolate, Father Rebagliati, all that was happening in Agua de Dios. The family was planning to attend. That night changed the destiny of Esteban's life.

Rebagliati's speech shocked the young Esteban enormously. In addition to seeking resources for the lazaretto, there was a need for who wanted to go and help the priests and nuns. There were no doctors. The religious communities were very small and lepers were arriving every day in abundance. He realized, then, how much he was longing to do something. Life could not be what he was living. There had to be more, and that was precisely what he was looking for.

After so much commotion over Rabagliatti's words, everything went back to normal. The Teatro Colón was full. All around him, he could only observe the hustle and bustle of the people. He could not believe that Rabagliatti's painful words were just the opening of mouths for yet another feast. The people began to dance, and with the dance they forgot about Agua de Dios. Everything was back to that frivolous atmosphere he was running away from: the same superfluous and repetitive conversations he already knew by heart. He waited until his father sat down at the table with his friends and Carolina was busy with her Sisters to secretly look for Rabagliatti. Esteban found him picking up his coat and begged him to help him do his final internship at the lazaretto. He told him he was a good doctor and that he was willing to leave that same week if he needed to. He had no obligation in the capital and felt he had a lot to give. Rabagliatti was at first very excited, but told him that it was important that he think it over and give it enough time. They agreed to talk about it again the following week, when he returned to the capital.

Esteban left the theater enraged, with a mixture of pain and impotence. He did not say goodbye. He simply left silently, invisible, in the midst of the people, trying to find a space in the half-light where he could sort out his thoughts and feelings.

By the following week, Esteban had already met with members of the clergy and the apostolate, and he had read the latest medical reports. He wanted to surprise Rabagliati and show him that his was not a whim or the desire of a passionate child. He wanted to prove that he was already a man and that his intentions were laudable.

Agua de Dios was a mystery, and that mystery made the adventure more exciting. Only certain circles knew what was going on there. His father, a member of these circles, also knew. That is why he never forgave him for going against his will.

Esteban left on an ordinary morning. He brought only a suitcase with his books, music, and some clothes.

He could not say goodbye as he would have liked. Neither Carolina nor his father ever accepted his decision. He took the train from the capital to Girardot. There he would begin his journey to the *city of martyrdom*.

9
The Call

I had been working on the documentary for months. I chose to separate myself from my friends and my social life. I could not do everything at once. I needed to concentrate. I only answered the phone when Diana called me, and sometimes I answered for Alicia, although Alicia had almost always already spoken to Diana, so I already knew what it was all about.

Then the rush began. I had to finish everything soon. I was still working on the interviews when Luis Antonio called. I found it strange, as he never called me. He scheduled me for late afternoon next day. I told him I still didn't have much to show for it, but that I was doing a good job. He replied that this evaluation was up to him alone. After hanging up, I immediately called Diana and told her I needed to see her. She invited me to dinner that same day—María Helena would be there.

After dinner, when Maria Helena left, Diana told me we needed to talk. She urged me to finish the story now. She told me that I had been writing for a long time and that she had to give Alicia a date. She also told me that Alicia and Luis Antonio wanted to make the story of Agua de Dios into a feature film.

I returned home. I sat down in front of the computer and went back to the story:

"...AND THE STORY goes back to the beginning of the twentieth century. It takes place in Colombia, in a small town called Agua de Dios, where the leprosy patients lived in confinement," says Luis.

Julio had arrived there, in 1907, when he was still a cleric. While doing his apostolate, he met and befriended a young lady, María, who had come to Agua de Dios accompanying her sick grandmother. María was an orphan and had only her grandmother. When her grandmother died, María was left in the care of the nuns. She also cleaned the nuns' house. Julio was especially fond of her. As her grandmother was a leper, people said that María was too, although this was never confirmed, but it was the way of thinking at that time.

Two years later Esteban arrived. Julio says that when he introduced him to María, they both fell in love instantly. From that love I was born. Then I was separated from my mother because she was apparently a leper and I was a healthy child. I spent my first years with my father, in the Salesian seminary.

Julio told me that during that time there were frequent confrontations between the police and the sick. In one of them, my parents, who were supporting the sick, died. I had no one. So, Julio decided to take me with him when his superiors sent him back to Spain after he had been ordained. With their help, I ended up in the orphanage in Salamanca. Julio also told me that he had suffered a lot in leaving me, but that he could do no more, and that he knew that I would be much better off in Salamanca than in Agua de Dios, because of everything that was happening there.

This was the story Julio told me that afternoon at Estrecho College. After that visit I decided it was time to put an end to the questions of my past. Julio had told me everything he could, and although I still had unanswered questions, I had found some peace in my heart. It was no longer worth looking back.

I continued to work and take care of my parents until my father became ill with cancer. Those months of illness were endless. My mother could no longer bear the suffering, watching my father perish in such a horrific disease. I divided my time between the office and my home, doing what I could, but I was tired. I gradually lost interest in things. I didn't even have the motivation to meet anyone. Loneliness was enough for me.

My father died almost a year after he was diagnosed with the disease. It was then that I officially became the head of the company. During that time I did a lot of traveling. I kept going back and forth, visiting customers and suppliers. This led me to have sporadic relationships in the places I visited, without any kind of commitment, and that is how I became lonely and bitter.

10
Julio & Esteban

ALFONSO CONTINUES reading in his dressing room:

Early the next morning, I took the train from Bogotá to Tocaima. The trip was not easy. The night before I had not slept at all. The situation with Carolina and my father was exhausting. I could not wait to leave.

At the station there was a white wagon that was used only by leprosy patients. There you could see the relatives saying goodbye with all the pain and grief you could imagine. It seemed as if they were being buried alive. There were policemen guarding the sick. People were running around, thinking they could be infected just by looking at them. Others looked on with hatred and resentment, believing it was all divine punishment for something they had done wrong in their lives. It was misfortune. I still remember the face of a child being forcibly separated from his parents, who were being taken away.

I couldn't believe it. I watched carefully everything that was happening around me. As I tried to sleep, my dreams kept coming back to that vivid image of the hooded man that made my nights bitter. In the last few days I had been having nightmares with the mysterious image of a hooded stranger.

I was startled awake by one of the ushers asking for my ticket. I saw through the window how we were leaving Bogotá—how I was leaving a life. I fell asleep during the trip. I needed to have enough strength to get to Agua de Dios. I knew that what awaited me there would not be easy.

When we were arriving at the Girardot station, I went to the bathroom wash my face with some water and dress properly. It was already getting late in the afternoon. Through the window I saw the image of a priest in a cassock. I knew he was the person who was coming for me, because Rabagliatti had already informed me. That's how I met Father Julio, or rather, Brother Julio, because at that time he had not yet been ordained.

Julio was from Madrid. He had been in Agua de Dios for two years. He was a young man, different from the stereotypical priest in our neighborhood. He seemed to be a man with many interests. He liked sports, hunting, music, and drinking. For me it was strange, accustomed as I was to Father Epifanio, who was a family friend and with whom I went to confession every fifteen days.

When I saw Julio, I felt I was doing the right thing. There, we both were, from such remote places, trying to do something for the world. Still tired, with the image of the always beautiful savannah landscape, I got off the train with a deep and belated feeling of reproach. I looked around for him, and among those traveling souls that were dispersed with the steam of the heat, I found that priest who greeted me with his hand. I came out of the wagon, frightened and scattered. I carried a suitcase in my hand, along with a jacket. In the other hand I held a handkerchief. It was very hot.

"Excuse me, are you Dr. Esteban Martínez?" asked Julio.

"Yes, I am," I confirmed. "You must be Father Julio."

"A pleasure," answered Julio as he gestured to give the suitcase to him.

"Please, just call me Brother Julio, since I have not yet been ordained."

"Well, you can also just call me Esteban, because I haven't graduated yet."

Julio and Esteban get into the carriage. Esteban looks calm, although he is a little shy. He carries his suitcase on his knees. The sounds of the carriage wheels and the snorting of the horses are the only things heard.

"How was the trip?" Julio asks.

"Very well. I didn't know it was so hot. It's my first time in this area."

"You'll get used to it."

"You're Spanish, aren't you?" asks Esteban with an ironic tone because of Julio's accent.

"That's right," Julio answers, smiling. "I arrived about three years ago. I'm the most recent. My colleagues have been here longer. The oldest is the superior, Father Evasio, followed by Father Luis Variara. You must know them."

"I know Father Rabagliatti," says Esteban. "In fact, he's the reason I'm here. I don't know Father Variara yet, but I've heard many things about him."

"They are both saints. Father Evasio, even, people in town call him the apostle of the lepers," Julio says with special pride.

After the station we continued our journey. It was about twenty kilometers. The horses were tired. There were few of them and they repeated this journey several times a day. It was a long, tiring, and slow trip. The sun was burning like never before. There were mosquitoes and we were thirsty.

We arrived at the *Puente de los Suspiros* (Bridge of Sighs) and there we stopped to rest. Julio got out of the carriage and invited me to join him at the bridge's railing. The breeze from the river seemed like a reward after the trip. Julio told me all about the history of the bridge, why it had that name, and what it meant in this area.

"Many people think that leprosy is a contagious disease," Julio said, looking toward the river.

"That's why when a patient is on their way there is a person in front of the carriage who announces it with a bell."

We continue our journey in a silent and reflective manner. We entered the mountain range and began the ascent. On the bridge, Julio had given me a first report on the general situation in Agua de Dios. It detailed the exact figures and the latest treatments that were being applied to the patients. It also talked about the budget, the government, and the laws. That was the first time I had access to the archives and undisclosed reports about Agua de Dios.

The town had 637 houses. Of that total, 120 belonged to the government and 517 had been built by the sick, with their own funds, on land ceded by the national government. There were five hospitals, where more or less 600 sick people were housed, and four asylums for children. There were also public offices, a school, pharmacies, and a bank. A total of 2,771 lepers lived there in isolation. It was the largest colony at that time.

We continued our journey, and as we passed, I could see how the children were hiding and the windows of the houses were closing. After a moment everything looked like a desert.

Behind our carriage came a man ringing a bell. In another carriage, behind him, came four lepers. Their cries could be heard in the distance. It looked like a funeral procession. Then we arrived at the main disinfection station.

I got off my horse without knowing what it was all about. All I could see were policemen and lines of people. Julio approached me and told me that everything would be fine and that it would be a quick process. A policeman approached me and told me to line up on the left side, along with other people who had been there for a while. To my right was a disgraceful scene.

Alfonso, stunned, continues reading:

I was shocked by what I saw. There was a middle-aged woman whose clothes were forcibly removed in front of everyone. Some were mocking her. The same policemen were throwing everything into a large chimney that kept on billowing smoke. The woman was screaming for them not to take away her suitcase, which contained her souvenirs, photos of her children, and her letters. The police threw everything into the fire, while the woman was consumed in an unwavering cry. They passed by, one by one, until the number was endless. Then, another policeman, with a hand on his nose, beckoned them into a room next door. There they began to bathe them all with large hoses.

"This is Dr. Esteban Martínez, the new doctor coming to help us," said Julio.

"Identification, please," said the commander,

"and then take your bag to my partner to check."

"Here they are," I said nervously, as I took out my papers and handed them to the commander.

"Where do you come from?" asked the man, looking alternately at the papers and my face.

"I come from the capital."

"You need two letters, doctor. The letter from the head doctor of the center and the permission letter for your admission."

"I have them here," I said, opening the briefcase.

"Before coming here, did you have contact with any leprosy carrier?" asked the commander.

"No, sir."

"Very well, then go to the bathrooms."

When it was my turn, the policeman asked me to take off my clothes quickly. I could not believe it… was this necessary? I was the doctor who came to see the sick. I replied to the policeman, with authority, that it was not necessary—but the policeman replied that it was, and also to watch my tone. I then realized that the place looked more like a prison than a place to take care of the sick. Why were there so many policemen there and why was the process so violent? I asked myself.

The humiliation could not have been greater. In the middle of the street, like animals on their way to the slaughterhouse, we were searched, groped, and even mocked. It was the first time I had taken off my clothes in front of someone. I was shaky and embarrassed. Julio noticed this—so he walked over and stood in front of me, trying to give me some privacy. I felt a mixture of anger and helplessness.

Once the inspection was over, we went to the bathrooms. There, against the wall, like a fugitive they had just found, they began to throw bursts of water at me that looked like cold stabs. Then the policeman threw my clothes back at me. I began to dress hurriedly, trying to get out of that painful room. Julio was waiting on the other side. Next to him were two women, also naked. Their faces were pitiful.
There was no hope in there.

There were few places like this one within the perimeter of Agua de Dios. They were placed in strategic locations. Their main purpose was to function as immigration offices. All those going in and out had to pass through them. It was the law. Those who left, had to leave their things, abandoned, to later be burned in the chimney avoiding any contact with the outside world. Those who entered, if they were healthy, had their clothes and belongings returned after the bath. If they were sick, then everything was taken away and burned. Visitors and patients had to carry a passport. Some had signatures of the presidency, and others had the signatures of the Directors of the leprosarium. On this passport was indicated the conscription status of the people and how they were to be treated because of their condition.

Upon arriving at the Salesian seminary, Esteban was warmly welcomed by Rabagliatti and the rest of the community. At that time only eight clerics, including the father Superior, formed the group.

"Welcome, dear Esteban," said Rabagliatti. "We were worried about you."

"Hello, father. Thank you very much," I replied. It took us a long time at the disinfection station. There were a lot of people.

"Brothers, may I introduce Dr. Esteban Martínez, who has just finished his medical studies with outstanding grades, and will do his final internship here at the hospital," announced Rabagliatti with a certain ceremony. "Esteban will be living with us. He is our new member."

"María, María!" shouted Rabagliatti looking towards the kitchen.

"Yes, Father, tell me," María answered.

"Please serve dinner for Dr. Esteban."

"Yes, Father, right away."

"Esteban, let me introduce you to María. She is in charge of the seminary kitchen. She lives with the Sisters of the Presentation. María arrived very young, accompanying her sick grandmother. When she died she had no one to be with. So she has lived with the Sisters most of her life. Whatever you need, you know she can help."

"Delighted, Miss María," I said. She nodded and left.

I settled in the visitor's pavilion of the building. My cell had a bed, a crucifix, a night table with a candle, a desk and a small chiffonier. It also had a small window, the main view of which summoned the treetops and the night stars. Behind the door was a poem by St. Teresa.

"It's not so bad. At least you have a window," Julio said to me, as he threw the suitcase on the bed.

"You don't have one?" I responded with a tone of surprise.

"We sleep on the other side of the courtyard. In this wing of the building are the superiors and the guests."

I opened my suitcase and began to put everything in order. I took out my books and put them on the desk.

Next to the books I placed a picture frame with Carolina's image.

"Who is she?" Julio asked, taking the picture frame in his hands.

"It's my fiancée," I replied, looking at the photograph. "She's a little upset about the decision I've made."

"And I see that you like music," said Julio, as he took out some sheet music from under the books.

"I used to play violin and I like write songs." I was a little annoyed by the number of questions.

"Very well. So, showers and toilets are down the hall to the right. Through this hallway you can go straight to the chapel. You saw where the kitchen and dining room are. Tomorrow morning I will introduce you to the Sisters of the Presentation, who are also forming their apostolate."

"Thank you very much, Julio. You are very kind."

"We are the ones who have to thank you. This is truly a gift from heaven and an answer to our prayers. I'll let you rest, tomorrow will be a long day. Good night."

Julio closed the door and left. I sat down at the desk and began to read the regulations and schedules that were observed every day in the convent. I read them carefully and immediately got to work, carefully reading the report of Dr. Pablo García Medina, a prestigious doctor whom I admired very much. García Medina had been conducting an investigation at the express request of President Reyes since 1905.

The next morning I woke up late. I did not understand where I was. I dressed as quickly as I could and went to the chapel to say the first prayers with the community, following the schedule that had been left on the table. However, I was already late. Everyone was at work. I grabbed some fruit from the kitchen and decided to leave for the hospital.

The Agua de Dios square was as crowded as a flea market. Outside the church there was a group of young people playing soccer. In front, a group of old people, sick, getting in some outside time in the company of the nuns. And on the corner, the one facing Real street, there was a group of men drinking and playing a game of *rana*. Father Evasio was coming out of one of the houses and I went to meet him.

"Father, good morning," I said, "It's good to see you."

"Good morning, son," replied Rabagliatti. "I didn't see you at morning prayers or at breakfast. Is everything all right?"

"Yes, father. Everything is fine. I'm sorry about this morning, but I was overcome by sleep. I was very tired."

"Don't worry. Come, walk with me, I want to show you what is most urgent."

Rabagliatti took me to the convent of the Sisters of the Presentation. At the entrance, a group of very sick lepers were lying on stretchers and being cared for by a nun.

"Esteban, let me introduce you to sister Josefina. She will help you get to know how the center works. Sister has been here for some time and knows Agua de Dios very well. She will explain what we have done so far and introduce you to the other doctors. There are not many of them, and they come only for days at a time." After saying this, Rabagliatti said goodbye and left.

I was bothered by what I saw. I approached the first patient, a young woman.

"What is your name?" I asked.

"Imelda, doctor."

"Well, Imelda, I'm Esteban. How are you feeling today?" I asked, brushing my hand over her face.

"Well, here I am, doctor. My body hurts a lot and I'm very hungry."

"Do you have a house or do you live in one of the shelters?"

"I live in the San Vicente shelter."

"And they didn't give you breakfast?"

"No, doctor. There is no food today. There will only be lunch."

I called Sister Josefina.

"Sister, what are you medicating the patients with?"

"I don't know, doctor," she answered somewhat nervously.

"I only do what they ask me to do. I don't know much about medicine and we give them what you give us."

"And where are the doctors? I don't see anyone."

"Most doctors don't come in for fear of contagion. They do their examinations from far away, through the barbed wires."

“What? This situation is not normal. These people are more malnourished than anything else,” I complained. “We have to talk to the health authorities about this. These are no conditions for a hospital.”

“You can talk to my superior, or to your superior. They can give you more answers than I can. We ask these same questions every day.

(Silence).

Now, if you have no more questions, I must leave to continue with my work.”

Josefina left the corridor, leaving me in deep thought.

THE NEXT DAY I prepared everything for the meeting with Luis.

Although his call had taken me by surprise, it was also true that I wanted to see him. I had many questions to ask. In the meetings, Luis said what he wanted to say and did not leave room for questions—but there were things I needed to ask him… It was time, and I had the confidence to do it.

I arrived at the appointed time and I sat down in my usual chair. After waiting for around 10 minutes,

Alicia came out of the studio to inform me that unfortunately Luis Antonio could not see me. It seemed strange to me—but I thought I would have more time to continue working. We agreed to meet the next day. I said goodbye to Alicia and returned home to continue writing.

That night I would meet Jorge for dinner in Zona-G. We had arranged to meet right after I met Luis Antonio. Jorge was adamant that we should do a special final interview with Luis Antonio, and I had had intended to ask Luis if this was possible.

I called Jorge and told him what had happened and suggested that we move our dinner date back a day. But Jorge already had plans then, so we met planned.

11
Music

After my father died, my mother's Alzheimer's progressed rapidly. Soon we were both total strangers. I was completely absorbed by work and my trips were getting longer and longer.

On one of those trips, I remember I was in Brussels, I got a call to tell me that my mother had tried to take her own life and that she was screaming her head off at home. This was the second time this had happened. It was then when I had to place her, with the deepest pain in my soul, in a geriatric hospital. There she passed away years later.

With my father dead and my mother mute in a nursing home, I concluded that the time had come to think about what I wanted to do with my life. I thought it would be best to leave Spain and perhaps return to Paris, a city that had taught me so much and which I knew very well.

I started to prepare everything. I left the business in order and sold some properties: the house in Madrid, the summer house in Comillas, and the land in the south. I planned to leave the following month, in May. Then I received a call from a stranger: Father

Julio had passed away and had left something for me. This took me aback.

The next day I met the stranger at a café in the Plaza de Oriente. We did not talk much. He only told me that it had been Julio's last wish that an envelope be given to me when he died. He also told me not to say anything to the Salesians.

I went home and opened the package. There were pictures and letters. One of the letter was from Julio to me. He told me that I should go to Colombia and see with my own eyes what was happening in Agua de Dios. Julio had already told me what he had experienced there. With my biological parents dead, I assumed I had no reason to make such a trip. However, with this letter, and I now thought that perhaps destiny wanted me to go to Bogotá instead of Paris. I wanted to leave Spain and I had everything prepared, so the change of destination should not be a problem, I thought. I immediately prepared my trip to Colombia and for my encounter with the past.

I wrote to the Valenzuelas, friends of my parents. I would stay at their house for the first few days. My idea was to arrive in Bogotá, rest for a couple of days, and then continue on to Agua de Dios, assuming that was even possible. I didn't have much information about Agua de Dios, only what Julio had told me in the Salesian school.

I didn't say anything about this to the Valenzuela' family, so as not to arouse suspicion. It would be quite strange that a Spaniard, who had just arrived in the country, would want to visit a town that was kept hidden and where people were not allowed to visit. I thought that the important thing would be to get to Colombia first. Once settled, I would figure out on my own how to get to my destination.

"I returned to Colombia, without being fully aware of it. The only memory that stayed with me was the knowledge that I had no family, no friends, and no past. The only thing I had was music. I grew up in Salamanca and Madrid with the vague memory that I had been abandoned in an orphanage and that a kind Spanish couple had adopted me." Luis says, while he returns to staring at the abyss of the window.

I arrived in Bogotá in 1957, at the beginning of August, escaping from the terrible summer that hit Madrid in those days. By the first week I had already met the Spanish ambassador, had two suitors, and had made friends with a couple of guys my age. Not bad at all, I thought. As I told you at the beginning, the Valenzuelas took me to every party there was.

I arrived in the country supported by a brilliant career in Criticism and Architecture. The Valenzuelas helped me get a job at the newspaper as a critic. In addition, I worked in the afternoons for the embassy, on the cultural side, promoting concerts. That's how I met Alicia. And that's how my plans to visit Agua de Dios became receded more and more.

We were working on the premiere of Manuel de Falla's *Noches en los jardines de España*. I had proposed the work in one of the meetings with the Cultural Committee of the embassy. It seemed to me that it could serve as an experiment to get to know the public in Bogotá and their aesthetic tastes. The following week, after approving the project, they called me to propose that I prepare the premiere and be in charge of everything. The responsibility was great, because the work was not only new for me and for the orchestra, but also for the conservative and traditionalist ears of the Colombian public.

The score had come into my hands through my father, who had friends in common with Falla. It had been composed around 1916, and although I was not myself a friend of Falla's, I felt close to the work. At some point I sought him out, but I learned that he had left for Argentina some time ago, escaping like many others from the civil war.

We began rehearsals with the orchestra in early November. Although we had no had not secured the pianist, the theater had already given us a date for December. At each rehearsal, the nationalism of the score transported me to Spain and brought back childhood memories. After my friend, the great virtuoso Juan de Armando, agreed to perform, we began the press work. My cultural work in Bogotá had inevitably pushed me to make peace with the European arts and styles of the time. After all, I was promoting Spanish culture and organizing recitals supporting new composers. We talked about all of this with the press.

The day of the concert, at half past six in the evening, I went to the hotel where Juan was staying. I needed to send some documents to Madrid, and Juan was doing me the favor, so we arranged to have a drink before arriving at the theater. Juan was impeccable to a degree I had rarely seen him.

At 8:15 the chords of the piece began. That night was magical. The dialogue between the Director, the orchestra, the piano, and the audience was amazing. Juan seemed like that lover who wanders in the darkness of the night of Cádiz. The audience gave a standing ovation until their hands were tired, and then I felt like a lucky man. I was grateful to the country and its people. Juan sat down again at the piano and, in gratitude, played Calvo's *Intermezzo No. 4*. In Madrid, Father Julio had told me all about Calvo, about his music, the *intermezzos*, and his life in Agua de Dios. I also knew that Calvo had been a very special person for him and for Esteban.

When Juan agreed to come to Colombia, I immediately looked for the score and gave it to him the same day he arrived. If he could prepare it in so few days, it would be the perfect gift for the Colombian public. And so it was. Juan prepared it without any problem.

Juan invited me to one of his rehearsals. That was when I heard the piece for the first time. That was also when I realized that this melody, which I had never heard of, was actually something I had heard before. This melody, I knew, was the same melody of my dreams. It was the music of those early years, the years of oblivion, the erased years.

Juan played it masterfully that night. The piano seemed to contain a deep sadness. The piece was warm; it produced a certain peace—a forgotten peace.

After the concert there was a dinner at the palace of San Carlos. I went into the dressing room to pick Juan up, while the theater slowly emptied. In the hallway, for a moment, I stared at the wall. Then I came to myself, wiped off the sweat, and continued. As we left, we noticed a woman waiting for us. She was small and slender, with a very tender innocence that quickly attracted my full attention. Her eyes not only expressed respect and admiration, but told me much more, although she was indifferent to me at the time.

"Congratulations on your wonderful interpretation of Falla," the woman said to Juan. I smiled, as if the compliment had been given to me.

"Where did you get the score of the last piece you played?" the woman asked.

Juan answered that I had given it to him, and that it was by a Colombian composer named Luis Antonio Calvo, whom neither of us knew.

"Do you know the piece?" I asked her curiously.

"Yes, I know it," she answered. "I like Calvo's works very much."

"Well, I would love for you to teach me more of his music," I said. "I don't know much of his work and this piece is quite peculiar. It has great meaning to me, so I would love to learn about his other works."

"Well, I'd be happy to do so. The day after tomorrow I have my painting class nearby, at the Bellas Artes. I finish around five o'clock. If you want, we can have a cup of coffee afterwards and talk some more."

"Well, there you go. I'll be there at five," I answered with a big smile. "What's your name?" I asked, intrigued.

"Alicia Turbay".

The night was cold. People had left for the palace in a hurry. I kept thinking about Alicia…

(Silence).

"I had been waiting a long time to tell this story, dear Leonardo," says Luis. "At eighty-five years old I could say that I have done and told everything but the truth. That's why I can no longer hide this story."

"And did you know him? Did you know Calvo?" I asked impatiently as I take notes.

"No, I did not know him," Luis answers. "When I arrived in Colombia, Calvo had already died. In fact, it was through Alicia that I was able to understand a little more about the enigmatic composer. I met Alicia two days later, as she had proposed. Alicia was unique. She was an independent thinking woman, way ahead of her time and ahead of the common women of that time in this country. She was very fond of art, especially painting. She also loved music and reading."

At that moment Alicia enters the studio, giving the impression of having heard everything.

"I heard my name from the hall. I suppose you're already telling Leonardo how we met," says Alicia, as she put a glass of water with a pill on Luis Antonio's desk.

"Don't believe everything he says, Leonardo. Luis loves to make up stories," she adds, as she left the study.

"So, then, who was Calvo?" I ask.

"You don't know who Calvo is?" says Luis Antonio with an astonished face. "Haven't you listened to his music? Something's wrong with you, kid."

"No, I don't know. The truth is that I don't know his music."

Luis Antonio stands up from his chair and walks over to his stereo. He takes out the CD that is playing, carefully puts it in its case, and places it on a shelf in alphabetical order. Then, a bit confused, looking at his extensive library and talking to himself, he manages to find another CD and puts it in. He returns to his seat. It was Calvo's music, played by a Colombian pianist.

"Calvo was a very well-known composer," Says Luis. "I think he was also a great pianist. He had a good reputation in the Bogotá society of his time. However, he was diagnosed with leprosy in 1916. This led him to seclude himself until his death in Agua De Dios.

"However, they say that his stay there was not as horrible as the rest of the people who ended up there," Luis continues.

"Calvo was famous, an important man, known for living the good life in the capital. He dressed, ate and drank well. He was always surrounded by the city's elite. He gave recitals in the homes of the wealthiest families and had their daughters as pupils. When his banishment was decreed, Bogota's society paid him a farewell tribute at the Teatro Colón. It is even said that, the day he left, all these women who were enraptured with him and his music were adorned with flowers and reserved a white carriage for Calvo and his entourage. A very different case from the rest of the ill, who were piled in a wagon, without light or windows, on their way to a land of no return. Calvo entered the lazaretto with a certain pomp, and there he waited for his piano, which arrived slowly, on the back of mules, along those crude and sultry roads."

"That's why Julio met him, in Agua de Dios!" I answers, exalted.

"That's right. Calvo was a friend of my parents and Father Julio. In fact, they say that they often met at his house. Apparently, Calvo would do recitals there—my mother would prepare dinner, and they would all share. I don't know if you realize, my friend Leonardo, but my name is the same as Calvo's."

I remained thoughtful. It was true, they shared the same name.

"And why is that?" I asks. "Is it just a coincidence or is there a connection?"

"Yes, there is a connection," Luis Antonio answers. "It seems that my parents had a deep appreciation for Calvo. And that's why they decided, in his honor, to name me after him."

"Now I understand why music is so important to you."

"And not only that. When my parents died and I was left in the care of the Salesians, Julio took me every morning to the Maestro's house, although we didn't go in, because I was a healthy child and couldn't have contact with a sick person. We only stayed outside, in the street. We would sit on the sidewalk, and then Calvo would open the window, a pink window, and play this and other pieces. Then he would wave his hand at us. I don't remember him. But I do remember the music and the window. After my parents' death, Julio was left alone and was never the same. Only the music of the Maestro comforted him."

(Silence).

"What happened after you met Alicia?" I asks, interrupting the silence in which the conversation had fallen.

"My life in Bogotá was then divided into two parts," Luis replies. During the day I was a detective looking to solve a mystery; and at night, a rich young European, visionary and industrialist, who enjoyed a good intellectual reputation and was looking for new horizons in the emerging South American lands.

Alicia interrupts the conversation. She has brought food.

I have been listening to Luis Antonio for hours. I am captivated by his story.

12
The Last Conversation

When I left Luis Antonio's house, my head felt like shit. There were so many intertwined stories that I was lost. Also, before I left, Luis told me that he wanted to make the story of Esteban and María into a film and that he knew I could help him. He told me that he had the right actor for the role of Esteban: Alfonso Santamaría. This baffled me.

I remember that I told him that was nonsense. Alfonso Santamaría, besides having a reputation for being conceited, unfulfilled, and complicated, was a bad actor. Yes, it was true that he had won a Goya Award and had become very famous, but the truth was that he had won because the role he played was precisely that of a conceited, alcoholic man with personality problems. In my opinion, Alfonso could only be good at playing the role of a shallow leading man. Besides, he was almost thirty years old, so I don't think he was a good physical fit for the character.

Luis didn't like my words at all and replied that if I didn't want to work with Alfonso, he would respect that, but then he would look for someone else to write the story.

I got home very late that night. I waited until the next morning to call Jorge and tell him everything that had happened. Jorge told me to stop by café Il Pomeriggio that afternoon, that he would be there with some clients.

The next day I told Jorge the story. I told him that it all made sense now. It was obvious why Luis wanted to do all this. It wasn't just the whim of a rich old man wanting to spend money, nor was it the altruism of a connoisseur seeking to help us discover our own history. This was his story and that's why he wanted to tell it.

We agreed that we would finish the documentary. The story would focus exclusively on leprosy and its repercussions in Colombia at the beginning of the century. Once finished, we would present it to different production companies and seek support from the culture ministry. Then, once the documentary was finished, we would go on to make a first script for the film, basing the story on the book Luis Antonio had written. I had not read it, but, according to Luis, it was a very complete manuscript. It was centered on the love story between Esteban and María, narrated from the political perspective of that time—that is, the abandonment of lepers by the

Reyes government, which was occurring just as Esteban arrived in Agua de Dios to do his medical internship. As for Alfonso, Jorge advised me to drop the subject. In the end, the problem would be for whoever directed the movie; and if the acting was not good, it would be the old man's money that was lost.

In the following weeks, I dedicated myself fully to giving shape to everything: the documentary and the first draft of the script. I had a lot of work to do, but more than a job, what I had was an obsession. I needed to finish everything and complete the circle. I had been working on this story for almost a year.

I sat at the desk, and began to shape the main dialogues between Esteban and Julio:

"Julio, Julio, Julio! Open up, please," Esteban murmurs from the edge of the door.

"What's wrong? Can't you see what time it is?" Julio answers, also in murmurs.

"May I come in?" Esteban implores.

"But why! We are already in *Silencio Absoluto*."

"What's that?" asks Esteban with curiosity.

"What do you want?" asks Julio in a hurry. I'm without my cassock. Tell me what you want and go away.

"I have to talk to you, even if it's just for a minute. I've been looking for you all day, but they told me you were out in town."

"It is not prudent for us to be seen here," Julio replies as he peeks his face through the small opening in the door. "Give me ten minutes and I'll meet you at the hospital door. I'll take you to a place where we can talk quietly."

Julio closes the little door and sits down on his bed. Behind him, standing naked, is María.

"What does the little doctor want now?" María asks Julio while she touches his hair with her hand.

"I don't know," he answers, buttoning his cassock. "You get dressed and wait. I'm going out and you're leaving."

"When will we see each other again?" asks María.

"I don't know, especially now with this boy here. He's just trouble."

"Trouble about what?" María asks, hanging on to his neck.

"You know what the problems are," Julio takes his hands off her roughly. "You must know what questions Esteban has."

"Well, he'll get used to it, like we've all gotten used to it," María rebukes him.

When Julio says goodbye to María, Esteban runs silently out of the seminary. He had heard everything. Julio follows in his footsteps. María remains naked on the bed.

Esteban and Julio meet. Everything is dark. Julio smokes a cigarette. He walks in a hurry, as if he doesn't want to be seen. He beckons Esteban to follow him and they walk off into the gloom.

After walking for a while, they arrive at a thermal pond. There are many bushes; the pond is behind them. Only frogs and crickets can be heard and steam from the pond can be seen.

"What a wonder! What is this?"

"My other shelter," answers Julio. "Come on, get in."

"It's ok. I just want a moment to talk. Besides, it's a bit late, and I don't have the right clothes to…"

"Let's talk, Esteban! No one will see us here, so you can tell me whatever you want. If you came at this hour for me, it must be because what you have to say is important. And as for your clothes, come on, boy, there's no girl around here, so don't worry about taking them off."

Julio starts to undress. Esteban looks at him in detail…

"What are you looking at?" asks Julio, surprised by Esteban's look.

"Nothing…" says Esteban avoiding the gaze.

"So? Weren't you in a hurry? Go on, get in!"

Julio begins to swim underwater. Esteban, meanwhile, takes advantage of the privacy and discreetly takes off his clothes, then inserts a foot to test the temperature. When Julio emerges from the surface and catches Esteban naked, he dives into the water in embarrassment.

"What a delight," commented Esteban.

"I told you. When the colonizers arrived, Jiménez de Quesada was in these lands. He was sick. They say he suffered from leprosy. He found these waters and, apparently, they helped him a lot. At least that is what the legend says. It was he who baptized them as "Aguas de Dios" (God's waters). There are several in the surrounding area. Sometimes I like to bring patients. Other times, I come alone. But, anyway, tell me, what's the matter with you?"

"I don't know how to say it," Esteban replied anxiously. "When I decided to come to Agua de Dios, I was full of illusions. I imagined Agua de Dios as a place of research, relief, and progress. But what I see is very different. Today I was visiting some patients who are under the care of the Sisters. I was very surprised at how malnourished some of them are. Also, I found people with no signs of leprosy. Aa lady named Imelda even told me that there are people who are only there to receive the government subsidy."

"Imelda is very gossipy. Don't believe everything she says.

(Silence).

"Look, Esteban, we are here to help and improve the lives of these people through what we do, with love," Julio replies. "Agua De Dios is very new. I can't imagine your face if you had seen what Father Evasio found at the beginning… "

Julio approaches the shore where they left their clothes. He takes out a box of cigarettes from his pants. He lights one and passes it to Esteban. Then he lights another one for himself.

"Look, only 20 years ago, the first Salesians arrived: Father Luis Variara, Father Evasio, and Father Miguel Unia. They say that the lepers were being driven out of the towns for fear of contagion. They say that in Tocaima they would not sell them food again, nor would they let them enter a store. That is why they were forced to leave. It was then that they came to Agua de Dios, which at that time was just an empty hacienda. And here they stayed. To be honest, it hasn't been easy. I also went through what you are going through now. All of us have to fight not only against the disease, but also against prejudice, indignity, humiliation, stigma. But, you see, little by little we are moving forward. We already have more shelters, a health center, and the Sisters are helping us a lot. Now, people, young people, have an illusion, a hope, and you are part of it."

"Why is it fenced off?" asks Esteban.

"Leprosy is not an easy subject," answers Julio. "People here have many beliefs and superstitions. We don't know the disease very well either. They say it spreads without you noticing it. At the beginning, patients were invited to enter the leprosarium of their own free will, but things got out of hand. The community was in danger and the patients were ignoring the measures they were supposed to take. So it was necessary to create this fence to prevent them from escaping. The sad part of it all is that now the patient loses everything, as enforced by law. It's like erasing your existence and your dignity in a second. I guess it is a legacy of the brilliant ideas left by your President Reyes.

"Is that the reason for the coscoja?" asks Esteban.

"Yes, it was more than necessary to circulate a coin that would not be manipulated by healthy people…"

They both remain silent. There is no need to talk any more. Julio lights another cigarette and passes it to Esteban. Then he lights one for himself. They lie down on the grass and stare at the starry sky…

AFTER FINISHING the documentary, I traveled to Los Angeles to work on the final editing. Before I left, I wrote an email, copied to everyone, outlining the plans to finish the project and suggesting dates to meet and review the footage once I got back from LA. No one replied to me.

Several days passed. We had already finished the final editing and the color correction, and we were preparing for the music recording. It was precisely that day, during the recording of Calvo's works, when I received the call. It was Diana. Luis Antonio had died the night before.

I put my hands to my face and was stunned. A few minutes ago I had been imagining what it would be like when Luis Antonio first saw our work and heard a recording of his much loved piano piece. My work had become a commitment to the old man, and if he was gone, I felt it had all been for nothing. I was devastated. I left the studio and went to the hotel. I drank a scotch and called Alicia, but I couldn't find her.

I immediately prepared to return the next day. I couldn't wait any longer.

When I got off the plane I called Diana. She told me that she had spoken to Alicia and that she had the details for the funeral. Luis Antonio would be at the funeral chamber that night and the next day he would be cremated. I got out of the cab, went into the house, changed my clothes, and hurried to the funeral home. There were few people, as if Luis had wanted some privacy in his farewell. He was a well-known man. I was surprised not to see more people. I entered the room and there I found Alicia. She was quiet. I sat down next to her and hugged her. Then she told me what had happened.

— JULIÁN DE LA CHICA

13
The Letter

Once he finished his year of internship, Esteban graduated with honors. He never heard from his family again. He wrote to his father frequently, but never received an answer. He tried to visit him physically, at first, but never got a positive response from them. He knew that Carolina was married and already had a child.

Alone and without obligations in Bogotá, Esteban returned to Agua de Dios after graduation. There he had his only family and his comrades in battle. He focused on his work day and night. He founded the Association of Itinerant Doctors, wrote for the local newspaper, and founded, along with Maestro Calvo, what would become a music school for children. He also continued his music lessons with Calvo and even played at some of his gatherings.

The infrastructure of Agua de Dios was rudimentary and lacked the instruments necessary to conduct adequate research. The Salesian Fathers, the Presentation nuns, and all medical workers struggled lack of food, safety concerns, vandalism, and overcrowding.

As time went by, groups of people began to appear in Agua de Dios who had been taken there by force.

Some, in tears, told how they had been persecuted and deprived of their homes, always without any kind of explanation. Agua de Dios was no longer big enough. The sick were few and the healthy many. The gross imbalance fostered strife, violence, and corruption.

By 1916, when Calvo arrived in Agua de Dios, Esteban had a notebook with a list that had taken him more than five years to make. It contained the names of people who, in his opinion, did not have leprosy. At that time leprosy was uncharted territory and you could lose your freedom just for having a little red skin, a scar, or a simple burn. Esteban was against these unfair procedures and encouraged his colleagues to perform a detailed analysis on patients before formulating reports that would seal their fates. However, many of his colleagues did not share his concerns.

Physicians were facing a credibility crisis, and many lost their jobs if it became known that they had treated a leper previously. At the same time, the police ordered, on behalf of the government, that physicians should lift the veal of professional secrecy when treating a leper. The authorities even threatened to sanction the entire guild if it was proven that doctors had covered up for someone who was infected. It was no different for priests. It was even said that they were obliged, in the *name of God*, to tell the authorities if a parishioner had confessed to them that they had the disease.

Esteban's studies showed that, after a certain period of time, many of these patients' spots disappeared without the need for any treatment. He was also surprised that a good number of these people had something in common: a history of political rebellion. Some were community leaders. There were also fugitives from justice.

Esteban's progress was slow. He had to wait months to confirm whether a patient had the disease. Because the sanitation in the shelters was so deficient, it also took him time to differentiate leprosy from a simple flu or allergies, to which the patients were vulnerable in the midst of so much poverty. It was not until the arrival of Adolfo León Gómez, a famous politician, jurist, and writer, that Esteban confirmed his suspicions. It was then that he decided to denounce what was happening.

Adolfo had been a magistrate of the Supreme Court, senator, and president of both the Colombian

Academy of History and the Colombian Academy of Jurisprudence. He was a wise and prudent man. His liberal ideas sent him to prison several times. Would Agua de Dios be his last prison?

Adolfo had arrived amid mysterious circumstances. According to his own account, in a Manizales newspaper, an article had been published stating that he had leprosy. Immediately the news circulated by word of mouth and Adolfo had to hide. When news like this came to light, people often went to the house of the supposedly sick person to force them to leave. On some occasions, depending on the mob, a mob would burn their home and belongings.

Adolfo feared for his life and that of his family. He knew that sooner or later the police would come for him and take him to Agua de Dios. So he decided to leave on his own free will and set out on the journey from the capital. But before stopping in Agua de Dios, he spent some time in the country house of some friends. It was called San Rafael, in Tocaima. There he would undergo a "novitiate," living in exiled solitude, to ease into the idea of entering the lazaretto.

That same night, Esteban met Julio and told him everything that Adolfo had told him: The stories of the panopticon (the prison he had been in so many times) and the speeches that made the government uncomfortable. Julio advised him to be cautious and told him that it would be best to talk to the doctors in Bogotá first.

The next day, Esteban sent the report and waited impatiently for a response. However, two months later he was called back Bogotá and told that reports had been received stating that he was trying to cover up for the sick. From that moment on, he was banned from working in Agua de Dios…

Madrid, November 15, 1954

Dear Julio:

If you are reading this, it means that I have already left to pay for my sins.

You don't know how happy I was to see you, to recognize you after such a long time and to find you a man.

I hope you don't hold a grudge against me. Here is all the information you asked for this afternoon. You have the right to know the truth. I would have preferred to do it in another way, in other circumstances, but I have always been afraid, even now that I am writing these lines to you. I am your father—not Esteban, as I told you during your visit.

I was shocked. I could not believe what I was reading. My head began to wander wildly, as I thought only of Luis.

At the funeral home, Alicia told me how Luis Antonio had died and about the folder he had given her with the documents. There was this letter that Julio had written to Luis, just after they met that afternoon at the convent in Madrid. Julio had not had the courage to confess his secret and preferred to wait until his death to tell everything. He entrusted the letter to a friend of his, preventing the congregation from reading it; and he made him promise that when he died, it would be given to Luis Antonio. Alicia never knew about it. She knew about it only after Luis died.

I continued reading aloud:

I fell in love with Maria, your mother, in a very innocent way. Life in Agua de Dios was not easy, especially for a young man who had arrived with doubts. The images I saw I could never erase from my memory. In María I found the family I needed. I was not able to live alone with such a weak vocation.

Your mother was an orphan. She had come to Agua de Dios at a very young age, accompanying her leprous grandmother. She grew up in the convent of the Sisters of the Presentation, where she also worked. Later, when her grandmother died, the Sisters took her in. She lived with them and spent her time helping in the convent's kitchen and in the Salesians' kitchen.

The first few years everything went well. Nobody knew about our relationship. María was a very noble woman and we both knew what we were doing. We were growing in our individuality, but we were doing it together. Since María was in charge of our food, it was not unusual to see her at the seminary all day. We lived our love without any suspicion being raised. Thanks to her I was able to survive those first months and be an example of virtue, as everyone said. What a saint

Father Julio is! What a blessing to have him with us!

We had been seeing each other for a while when Esteban arrived. The year was 1909. When I met him at the train station, I realized that we would be great friends. I introduced him to María and then told him the secret. Esteban never judged me. He was an open, visionary, compassionate person. He was only twenty-two years old, but his mind seemed like that of a fifty-year-old man.

But time passed and Esteban also began to feel lonely. It happened to all of us. Old and young, we were all going through the same experience. At the beginning it was all expectation and a desire to work. We aspired to be saints, to make a difference; but as the months went by, we grew tired and even lacked faith. We doubted God's mercy; how could we alleviate the pain of those oppressed, if what we wanted was to alleviate our own? The lepers thought that we had come to heal their wounds, to help them to find God in their suffering, but they did not know that it was they who were helping us to find the God we proclaimed so much.

I became Esteban's father confessor. I knew his innermost secrets: his fears, his doubts. I knew why he had come from the capital; I knew his past and his history. I also opened up to him.

Then one night it happened. We were celebrating the priestly ordination of some brothers in Italy. There was a big dinner at the seminary and we drank that night. It was not the custom. We drank too much and, without realizing it, the early morning caught us hugging each other, asleep, next to each other, next to the river.

That filled us with fear and shame. But none of us said anything. We stopped talking to each other for a few days, something unusual in our friendship. Esteban distanced himself, and I understood that it was a way to protect himself and also to protect me. How could I have disorderly love affairs with another man, being a servant of God?

Days passed, but I still had the memory of his naked body on top of mine in my head. I could still feel his smell and his hands caressing my hair. I decided to talk to him and called him back to the pond. From there you could see the town and it was easy to tell if someone was coming. I told him that we had to talk, that we could not stay like this.

Esteban arrived at the appointed time, but before we said a word, we were already rolling around in the grass like lovers who can't wait any longer. That day we didn't talk. Our encounters started to become frequent. We were fucking like animals. I thought that what I was experiencing was perhaps a carnal issue that did not involve love. I even thought it was a vile aberration that could only happen in that unfortunate town. But I was wrong. Forbidden love is attractive because it has a hint of madness wrapped in lust. Esteban became my obsession, and with him in my head, I no longer cared about María.

The year that Maestro Calvo arrived was, perhaps, the happiest in my life and in Esteban's life. The Maestro was well known in the country. When he was diagnosed with leprosy, the Bogotá society, in recognition of his art, gave him a house with a piano in Agua de Dios. From then on, every night there were dinners and get-togethers. Calvo knew about our story, and Esteban and I could be at ease when we met at his house.

But one night everything I had feared happened. María, sneaking through the corridors, waiting to reach my bed in the hours of the morning, surprised Esteban and me naked and hugging. From then on, her eyes lost their sparkle and her soul withered…

I promised María that I would never see Esteban again and that it had been a complete mistake and that we had no reason to talk about it again. Then, she threatened to tell everything if I didn't formalize a relationship with her. She told me to run away from Agua de Dios and to leave the priesthood. She said that Colombia was big and that we could start a new life somewhere else. I, on the other hand, only thought about Esteban. I began to see María again, but my heart had a different owner.

When Adolfo León Gómez, an important politician in the country, arrived at the lazaretto, things changed. Esteban had been conducting investigations into the health, budget, and corruption surrounding leprosy drugs. He had a list that he had compiled over the years. They were names of people living in Agua de Dios who were not leprosy carriers. Some only had stains, others were there because of the subsidy the government gave them, and others, like Adolfo León, remained there because their speeches made the government uncomfortable and they had to be silenced. Esteban's conclusion was that Agua de Dios had fallen into disgrace and there was no one who could control it.

The list soon became a threat to some, including Esteban himself. He had sent his reports to the Medical Committee of the Lazarettos, but he was neither heard nor well received. On the contrary, he was silenced. In less than a month, Esteban was removed from his duties at Agua de Dios and forbidden to practice medicine. According to them, he was conspiring and covering up for the sick, forming and encouraging rebellions against the government.

Esteban and I fell into a deep sadness. We could not live without each other and we were all we had. If he had to leave Agua de Dios, I was willing to follow him. But where would we go? We had no money, no job, no friends, nothing. So that night we made a plan.

of revenge. This included women as well as men who were raped by other men.

In the following months, while accompanying María during her pregnancy, Esteban began to decline in health. We did not know what was happening. Zacarías, a physician friend, said he did not understand his deterioration. Esteban was barely thirty-three years old; he was young, healthy, athletic. Zacarías told me that the best thing to do would be to call his relatives and take him to Bogotá. But I knew that Esteban had not spoken to his father since he had arrived in Agua de Dios. We were all he had.

María decided to forgive Esteban and took care of him. In this way I could continue the apostolate and fulfill the responsibilities of the monastery. With Esteban in bed, María pressuring me and the sick coming in, I felt that I no longer wanted to live. That was not the life I wanted. And that was not the God I believed in and wanted to serve.

The day you were born was perhaps the happiest day of my life, as well as the most miserable. I was filled with so much love at the sight of you that I felt as if my heart would burst with happiness, but at the same time I felt like the most wretched and selfish man. What future could I offer you in the circumstances I was in?

Hopeless and bored with life, I became a silent and sad man. I would spend long hours sitting on Esteban's bed while he slept. I would read and try to pray, but the truth was that I no longer believed in anything. I was not afraid either.

When you turned one month old, María told me it was time for me to keep my word. I knew that day would come and that sooner or later I would have to respond to the commitment I had made to her. However, I had changed my mind. I had concluded that this would be madness. I could not go through life lying and María did not deserve to live in misfortune.

The next day I spoke to María and told her my plans. I told her it would be best if we stayed just as friends. I made it clear that I would take care of you, but that I would not live with her, because I did not love her. She felt ridiculed and reacted violently to my words, vowing that she would take revenge on me.

I went to bed early that night. I was anxious. I knew María would go and tell everything to my superiors. It was only a matter of time. But I was not afraid, at least not anymore. The only truth that could never be known was my love for Esteban. The rest didn't matter to me. The next day I went to look for María, but I was told she had left. For several days, I didn't hear from her or the baby. I thought that maybe she needed some time and that was why she had moved away. I decided to wait and not pressure her. I knew that all this was too much for her.

The following week, one night, I was beginning to say my prayers as usual, before going to sleep, when I heard people shouting. I put on my cassock and hurried out. From the square I could see that one of the shelters was on fire. People were screaming for help. I did not understand what was happening. An all-consuming feeling came over me. I was just begging for the flames not to becoming from the shelter where Esteban was. When I arrived I saw María, like a madwoman, screaming and crawling on the floor begging for forgiveness. The flames were coming from Esteban's shelter. "Where is he?" I wondered. I could see everyone but him. The shelter began to fall apart. I tried with all my might to enter, but I could not. I knelt down in front of it and cried. I cried like I have never cried before. Of all those who were in there, Esteban was the only one who did not have the strength to get out of the shelter.

María disappeared that night. A few weeks later her body was found by the river in the next town. Jaime, one of the patients who slept near Esteban told me everything. He told me that that night, when María went to bring Esteban his medicine, the two of them had had an argument. Apparently, Esteban had told María that he knew she had been poisoning him for months and that this was the reason for his physical deterioration. But he forgave her, because he would rather die than become a problem for me. Esteban was sure that I would not abandon him and that this love would become my perdition.

Without Esteban and María, now the only thing that mattered was you. I decided to clean everything up and make the story presentable. I told people, especially Imelda, the town gossip, that Esteban and María were lovers and that he was your father. I also told them that María had not told them out of fear, because she knew that, as the father was a leper, the son would be immediately sent for adoption. To Jaime, the patient who had heard everything, I said that Esteban was very sick and that everything he had said to María was just a delusion. I further explained that Esteban had died of leprosy and that the idea of poisoning was complete madness. The news soon spread to the neighboring villages.

I confessed to my superior that I was your father and that I had been involved with María for several years. I also told him that I understood that the best and most reasonable thing to do was to leave the congregation. But my superior replied that this was not possible. The congregation was relatively young, new in Colombia, and it would be seen as a scandal. He told me that he would help me give you a future if I decided to continue and not tell anyone else. That was why, even though I no longer wanted to be there, I agreed to stay, to pay my penance and thus to free you from a painful fate.

You lived with the Sisters during those first years, while I was finishing my theology studies. During that time, whenever I could, I took you in the mornings to the Maestro's house to listen to him play his piano. That was the only memory I had of Esteban.

Later I was ordained in Bogotá. After that I was authorized to return to Spain. I went with you, as I had agreed, with the commitment to find a family for you. You know the rest.

That is your story, Luis. And that is my story. Never doubt you are the fruit of love. Because if anyone loved, it was me and Esteban.

Julio.

I closed the letter with deep sadness. Now I understood why Luis Antonio lived tormented by his past for so long. I could only imagine how difficult it would have been for someone his age to live with this torment. Today, times have changed, and yet we still see repudiation, homophobia, lack of acceptance. How could this old man, raised in postwar clerical Spain, live with the burden of such knowledge? How could he handle the burden? I immediately called Alicia and asked her to meet me the next day. We had to talk, and there could be no more secrets.

That night I did not sleep. I felt that I was an accomplice to something. Something I didn't understand, but I knew I had to let go, because this story didn't belong to me. I went to the kitchen, poured a glass of whiskey, and rolled a joint. I thought about doing a line as well, but decided against it. I sat down at the desk and started reading it all from the beginning. I realized then that there were so many, so many mistakes. I thought that maybe it was because of my mediocrity that *Carlota la puta ingenua* had not had any success; maybe I was telling everything half-heartedly. How could this story tell the truth if I was leaving out the most important thing?

I had so much information in my head that I decided to do nothing. Maybe the story had been told that way, because Luis had wanted it that way. Maybe the art had predisposed it to be that way. Maybe it was not in my hands… I spent a couple of hours reading and rereading, until I went to bed. There I waited, awake, waiting to meet Alicia.

14
Alfonso & Alejandro

I fell in love with Luis Antonio the night I met him. Unfortunately, he couldn't return the same sentiment to me. We became good friends and later he offered me a job. I became his everything. I became his maid, his secretary, his friend, and sometimes his mistress.

I moved in with him. Then he told me part of his story, the same one he shared with you at the last meeting. I never knew the whole story. I understand that Luis had his reasons for not telling me. I suppose it was out of embarrassment, or simply because he didn't want to share it with anyone. I don't know for sure.

When his parents died, Luis faced great depression and loneliness. He felt abandoned and hopeless again. That feeling, which he had been running away from for so long, came back with more strength. He decided to sell everything and move back to Paris, where he would take up writing again, which was what he was most passionate about. However, his plans were cut short when he got the call. Julio had died.

A stranger told him that they should see each other soon, because he had something for him. So Luis received the letter, among other things. The stranger handed him an envelope. There were pictures of Agua de Dios, a picture of Esteban, another picture of all of them together in church, music scores, and a drawing: I think it was a portrait of Esteban.

When Luis read the letter, he immediately organized the trip to Colombia. Now more than ever he wanted to get to know Agua de Dios.

"What was that encounter like?" I asked impatiently.

"It wasn't as soon as he had planned," answered Alicia.

Although at that time Agua de Dios was no longer like it was in Julio and Esteban's time, it was still a fenced-in place and there was a ban on visiting it. The infamy of being a concentration camp where all kinds of horrendous experiments were practiced had grown over time. What was once a secret in small circles was now public knowledge.

The visit to Agua de Dios did not take place until February of the following year. Luis had been in Bogotá for about six months, and I had been living with him for a little over a month. I arranged the meeting. I spoke with the Salesians and told them, according with Luis instructions, that we had a donation from Spain. We also told them that we knew about their work thanks to Father Julio. It was not difficult to coordinate the visit.

On the day of the trip Luis Antonio was very nervous. I had never seen him like that. During the whole course we didn't talk and he didn't let go of my hand. I remember that the way was long. There were still marked wagons, where they took the lepers. They still used the wagon with the horses that took you from the station to the entrance of the town.

In Agua de Dios things went well. At least better than I expected. We spent part of the afternoon with the Salesians, remembering Julio, sharing stories. Then they took us on a tour of the town. We visited the shelters, the hospital, the convent, and the cemetery. We also went to the house of Maestro Luis A. Calvo. That day we met his wife, Ms. Ana de Calvo. We asked the priests if there were still people who had known Father Julio, and indeed there were. One of them was Imelda. When we heard her name, Luis told me that we had to talk to her. We told the priests that we would like to meet her, and I took it upon myself to entertain them so that Luis could talk quietly with the woman.

"Imelda, I would like you to tell me if you know where Esteban is buried, the doctor who died in a fire and who was a friend of Father Julio," Luis asked.

"You see, sir, I don't remember that anymore," she answered. "It's been many years. I do remember the father, but I'm too old to remember the rest."

"Look, I'm going to leave you some money so you can be well and have a decent retirement," Luis said. "Nothing is going to happen to you. I'll talk to the priests myself. I just want you to tell me what you remember," Luis begged, as they sat down on a park bench.

"That story was so weird," she said, as she looked at the envelope with money in it.

"I know. Tell me what you remember. I won't tell anyone," said Luis.

"Well, the priest was involved with a young woman, María, the one who used to feed the priests," said Imelda in a low voice. "They lasted a while, until Doctor Esteban appeared, and then things got complicated, because the young priest also got involved with him. Oh, God! A very strange thing."

"What happened next, Imelda?" Luis asked.

"Well, they went on like that for a long time, until María couldn't take it and to make the young priest feel bad she told him that she was expecting his child. I really don't think it was his. In town we knew that young María liked the streets and that she had her 'friends' out there. You understand me, don't you?"

"And then?" Luis asked.

"Well, that didn't help either. Those boys kept seeing each other. Then poor María, in desperation, visited Etelva, the witch. You know, the one who lives in the cemetery. She gave her a potion to give to the doctor every night under the guise of medicine. And so she did. The girl, innocent, out of love did what the witch told her. But the potion had no effect. Those boys continued seeing each other. But who knows what was in that drink, because the boy got sick. He was skinny, almost like a skeleton. Some said it was because of leprosy, but I didn't think so. He was yellow and without strength. He lived sleeping and complaining of pain, and he was so handsome! Poor thing."

(Silence).

Then the woman gave birth and a boy was born. And those poor people didn't know what to do. The little boy was with the Sisters, the other one was trying to take care of the doctor, and, well, that's what they were doing until the fire happened.

"Do you know how it happened?" Luis asked.

"Of course I do," said Imelda. "I was there. It was at night. The girl had been bringing the food to the doctor for some time. Then she would come back for the dishes and give him the medicine before going to bed. That night it seems they had an altercation. And it was strange, because that week she had gone to Tocaima, so during those days, nobody saw her, not until the night of the fire. That's what Jaimito told me; he who slept in the bed next to the doctor's bed. The girl told the doctor that she and Julio were going to leave, but Julio didn't know how to tell him. That boy got upset and called her a murderer. He told her that he knew she was giving him "something" at night. But that he was at peace, because soon he would depart and leave Julio in peace. Although he assured her that he would not leave without first telling Julio what she had done, so that he would know what kind of person she was. When the girl heard that, she went crazy, grabbed a pillow and put it over the doctor's face, as if she wanted to smother him. People got up desperately to help. Amid all this struggle, the candle on the night table fell and the flames quickly devoured the shelter. Little was left of the boy."

"Did Father Julio know all this story?" Luis asked.

"Of course. I told him myself. Then the father asked Jaimito if what I had told him was true, and he confirmed it. Then they made up a lot of stories, that the doctor was the boy's father, that they were lovers, etc. What did it matter if the doctor and the girl were dead? She jumped off the bridge. She was found a few weeks later. She couldn't stand the grief of the young priest and what she had done. Well, that's what some people say, because there were those who said that she had actually escaped, that she was in Tocaima, where she had gone to look for her other son."

"Another child?" Luis asked with surprise.

"Well, the eldest. The girl María had another son. The thing is that they gave him up for adoption to a family in Tocaima. It was never known who the father was. I already told you that María was quite a free spirit with men."

"Imelda, do you happen to know the last name of that family in Tocaima?" Luis asked anxiously.

"Yes, the Restrepos," Imelda answered. "A famous family of politicians."

The priests began to get impatient with Luis and Imelda's conversation, and I could no longer make up anything else to hold them back. So we went to where they were and I told Luis that it was time to go. We said goodbye to the priests and Imelda and started our return trip.

On the way, Luis told me everything that Imelda had told him, or at least what Luis wanted me to know at that moment, because when I read the book I knew that Imelda had told him much more than what he had told me that day. Luis told me that it was important for us to find out which family had adopted María's son. He also asked me to try to find the son's whereabouts. I told him that was nonsense. No one was going to give us that information. We didn't know if the parents were alive and, if they were, they would never tell us the truth. That same day I managed to get Luis to forget about it, to look to the future and to live. He had already done too much and had enough suffering in his life to add more. What he needed to know he already knew. The rest was no longer important.

The years went by. I can say that we had a relatively quiet and happy life. Luis had decided to settle in Colombia and open a foundation with the money from the sale of the shipping company he had inherited from his father. The work of supporting new talents through the foundation and writing kept him active and busy. I, for my part, took care of all his affairs: investments, meetings, expenses, doctor's appointments, everything. But one day the past crept back in. It was 1990, and Calvo's wife, Ana, had died.

We had promised ourselves not to return to Agua de Dios. We even felt annoyed when we had to go to Girardot or Tocaima. But Luis changed his mind and decided to go to the funeral. Things had changed then. It was no longer the Agua de Dios we had known twenty-five years before. Imelda had died and the town was a normal place, full of fruit trees around it. Ana left in her will the desire to give the house to the town in order to preserve the memory of the Maestro. The only condition she made was that it be kept the same as it was when he lived there. When Luis found out about this, he asked the Director of the Cultural Center, after the burial, to take him to Calvo's house. He told him that it was important to see the state it was in and to know if work needed to be done or if it was necessary to bring in experts to catalog the music. In addition, he offered to help and to recruit others to help with the work.

The gentleman took us to Calvo's house and Luis sat on the sidewalk, just like when he was a child. The window was still pink and time continued to stand still there. We entered the house and Luis began to see everything. In the corner, next to the piano, was the Maestro's cello. Luis opened it, put it on a chair and began to review what was in the case. Then some sheets of music in a small pocket caught his attention. He took them out and put them on the table. The mystery had been unraveled. Luis found what appeared to be the first page of sheet music he had played when he was child. It was the same music and the same writing. It had no title, but it did have a dedication: "For Julio, with all my love. If loving you is a sin, let such a precious misfortune fall on me." There was also the charcoal drawing. It had been painted by Julio for Esteban on his last birthday.

I would say that that day was perhaps the first day that Luis slept in complete peace. This music had planted in him, when he was just a child, a question that had followed him all his life and had led him to search for his story and never rest until he found it. Then, later, the music came back to break the silence and rest. How curious, I believe, music somehow took him to that orphanage, and that score was known to him when he was just a child. Then the same score would return so many years later. How ironic, don't you think?

Luis assumed that Julio had wanted to get rid of the music page to prevent anyone from seeing the dedication; he left the page at Maestro's house. He did the same with the drawing. Maestro would keep the secret, although it is not clear to me if he even knew about it.

The return to Agua de Dios revived the memories of his brother. Luis wondered again what had happened to that family and where they were. I insisted that it was not a good idea. But Luis was a stubborn man. When he got an idea in his head, no one could change it.

When we returned to Bogotá, Luis hired an investigator to help him get the information he was looking for. He just wanted to know what had happened to this person, if he had family, and where he lived. Within a month, the investigator got all the information, something that brought a lot of clarity to the case.

With those only two clues that Imelda had given Luis, the agent found Joaquín and Teodora Restrepo, the only family in Tocaima that were politicians and with that surname. When we saw the records, the surprise was even greater. In 1909, Mrs. Teodora had had a son. The strange thing was that, in that year, the lady was more than sixty years old. It was evident that the little boy who was registered as her son, and whom they called Alberto, was not a biological son. We also discovered through the investigator that the children of leprosy patients had their parents' identity erased from their records. The pieces fit together. That child had to be the brother of Luis.

Upon further investigation, we realized that unfortunately none of them were still alive. Alberto's parents, as well as his siblings, had died many years ago. Alberto was the last one, but he had been dead for two years. Alberto was known to have been married to a woman from Tolima named Ana Milena, with whom he had two children: Carlos and Inés. Carlos had died in an accident when he was sixteen years old. Only Inés was left; she was married to another politician, Pedro Santamaría, with whom she had a son, Alfonso.

In the following months, Luis was calm. I think he had a feeling that little by little the pieces of the puzzle were coming together. However, the following year the sadness returned: Pedro, Alfonso's father, was assassinated.

It was the time of Escobar and the cartels. Insecurity reigned in the country, and Alfonso's father was a strong critic who supported extradition. His murder was a tragedy that Alfonso, his son, was never able to overcome. No wonder he leads such a tormented life, with such pain.

Now I know that Pedro's funeral was the only time Luis was close to his biological family. On that occasion I was not willing to accompany him, and the whole idea seemed crazy to me. Luis persuaded me, saying that Pedro was a well-known man and that many people loved him and would accompany him to his last resting place. He told me that our presence would not even be noticed in the midst of so many people. So I agreed.

That day, in the cemetery, in the midst of sadness, Luis saw Inés and Alfonso.

After the tragedy, in the following years, we did not hear from them. The only thing we knew was that they had gone to live outside Colombia and that they hardly ever came to the country.

"Alicia, are we talking about the actor?" I asked in deep surprise.

"Yes, that's right, answered Alicia.

"How did you know he was an actor and how did you hear about him again?" I asked.

"Relatively recently we found out everything Alfonso was doing," answered Alicia.

It was by chance. I was sitting with Luis, drinking a brandy after dinner and watching television, as we usually did. Suddenly they announced an interview with Alfonso, promoting *Ermenegilda*, the soap opera in which Alfonso had his debut leading role. Right then, Luis realized that Alfonso's face was similar to Julio's. I remember Luis said: "But he looks just like Julio when he was young. He looks like a portrait." I didn't know what he was talking about. Also, it was obvious through his last that Alfonso was the son of Inés and Pedro. But there was a curious thing: In one of those midday interviews, Alfonso was wearing a medal that was identical to one that Luis had. It was a Salesian medal. This was the first time we had seen Alfonso as an adult.

After reading the book, I connected all the dots. Of course I understood why Luis was so obsessed with finding the identity of his brother. Also I learned that

Luis had concluded that day, in the Alfonso's TV interview, that Julio had also been Alberto's father and that his great-grandson was proving his suspicion. What it also allows us to understand, my dear Leonardo, is that Julio and María had a very long relationship.

From then on we followed him. Luis thought that Alfonso should know the story of his biological family, his great-grandparents, María and Julio, and Esteban and of him, his great-uncle. Luis felt so proud! He longed to hug him, to tell him that he was his great-uncle.

Those were different times, and with today's technology it would been much easier to try to contact him. However, we looked for him several times, especially when we heard he was visiting Colombia, but he never agreed to see us. After the award his fame grew and he lived surrounded by people. It was impossible to get to him. This greatly saddened Luis, a man who was not used to being treated badly. Luis was a discreet and low-profile man. All the celebrity pomp in which Alfonso lived seemed ridiculous and disproportionate to him.

But one night, watching an interview in which he was talking about his award and the film he had worked on, he mentioned that what interested him most about a project was when the character he had to bring to life was pushing him to his limits. That really stuck with me. At that moment I thought about Agua de Dios and the stories that were still untold. All we had to do was research, put the pieces together, and tell a story.

Luis didn't like the idea very much at first, but then he ended up accepting it. Sooner or later we would get to Alfonso. He would agree to make the film and Luis would tell him everything.

We started the project and it wasn't difficult to find you, because when we asked who could be the right person to make the documentary, several people referred us to you. So here we are, and the rest I think you already know.

After Luis died, I read everything and I understood that Luis' own life was the story, and that I had to finish it. The only secret we must keep is the love triangle. I don't think it's up to us to tell that story; let Alfonso tell it if he wants to, when he wants to. In the end, it is about his own family and history.

Now you know everything, dear Leonardo. And now that we are starting the shooting, I will complete the promise I made to Luis the night he died. I will go to Alfonso and tell him the truth. I will leave him Esteban's letter and his great-uncle's book. Alfonso Santamaría deserves to know everything that his great-uncle discovered throughout his life, in addition to the inheritance he left him—and his story, which is the most valuable part of his life.

"THERE HAVE BEEN many stories of thousands of anonymous Colombians who disappeared in this era, against their will and banished from their lands. All those who had the divine punishment arrived in this city. The stories of a concentration camp that they want to keep in oblivion are yet to be written," Luis says, as he reads his manuscript out loud.

There is silence in the room. I do not know what to say. But that is already customary.

"By the way," Says Luis.

"Do you remember that I told you about Tomás, the first person I met with leprosy?"

"Yes," I answered. "The brother of Isabel, 'one of your young loves."

"Well, he didn't have leprosy. He was homosexual. When his parents discovered it, they preferred to say that his son had leprosy, to say that he was… 'different'… It seems that he had a lover that he would meet in the hills. From there came legends about the Monserrate's monster and its victims…

Tomás committed suicide. He cut his wrists with pieces of the bottle of rum I brought him… There isn't a day that I don't remember him. His ghost lives here… He is always with me…"

(Silence).

It is 11:24 p.m. on any given day. The music evokes the images of a movie, whose premiere, in a theater in Rome, reminds me of loneliness. The fireplace is lit. Every day, at eight o'clock, Alicia lights it. Now I sit writing, remembering and inventing a story. A light dew falls on the window to my left. The night seems to want to be silent. Neither can the wind be heard.

The image of the clock takes me to the old bell tower of Agua de Dios. It is half past three in the morning. The square is empty. I only see some lights on in the security sentry boxes around the town. Someone comes out of one of the corners of the square. The music continues mysteriously, intertwined with the sounds of crickets and the movement of the trees.

AGUA DE DIOS IS SILENT. The dawn is on its way. The candlelight makes the window of Esteban's cell visible. Still awake, he continues to write:

> *I've had some visions in the last few days. They terrify me.*
>
> *I am cold and walk in the dark, surrounded by faces judging me and criticizing me for what I have done. The halls have a reddish hue. I know them. I have walked them for so long, but I am still afraid. I long for the comfort of that in whom I do not believe. I long for the dirty, smelly, stagnant water outside your door. The emptiness fills me. I have anguish and forgetfulness. I feel sweat on my hands that no longer feel. Everything is gone and time has taken everything from me, even the memory of oblivion. I am proud to think that my shadow sculpted misfortune and banishment, but these are only the feelings of a defeated man.*

The door of the chapel is next to me, open. I can see the figure of sleeplessness. It is death and it is bread. It is the kiss of the third night. It is sin and it is devotion. I breathe with difficulty. I walk slowly. The figure is kneeling, penitent and waiting. I approach and caress it. I know who it is and I know it. I kneel beside it.

I clasp my hands tightly together. I do not pray to plead, but I clasp my hands together. I want to see it. I want it to look into my eyes and put its hand on my chest. Time is no more. It is not. It does not exist. It's just the two of us. I face my destiny. Then it stands up. It looks me in the eyes. That must be it, I think. It puts it's hand on the middle of my legs. I feel relief and lust. I do the same and feel hope. The false comfort of the voiceless. The scorn of the walking woman.

I look into its eyes, and then slowly remove its hood. The poet who is silent has shared its story. It' has told me what should not be told. It only watches patiently and listens in the silence of the innocent.

I think this is a punishment. A punishment for loving a man; for loving another man; for loving a servant of God. But what punishment it is.

I don't know if I should write this to you... I don't want to get you in trouble with the priests. But I felt a bit of energy today, after seeing the Maestro, and I thought: What if I'm not here tomorrow to tell you? If I leave tonight, then you may never know that I loved you?

I am silent and wait. I am quiet, asleep, remembering you in my dreams. I covet the morning to see you again.

It is useless to think that we can go back to the beginning of everything, without feeling that we are throwing ourselves into a fatuous and desolate void that devours you in the attempt.

E.

I AM EIGHTY-FIVE years old. I never married, I live in the company of Alicia, my nurse, friend, and confidant. I have a cat I call Bach, a watch that reminds me of the end, a drawing that brightens my days, music that has never forgotten me, and I have, especially, God's Punishment. It is useless to think that we can go back to the beginning of everything, without feeling that we are throwing ourselves into a fatuous and desolate void that devours you in the attempt.

Luis Antonio Gómez-Muñoz.
Bogotá, June 11, 2000

ALFONSO CLOSES the book written by Luis Antonio, which Alicia gave him the day he started shooting. He is sitting in a coffee shop in Los Angeles when he finishes it. It is a very beautiful day. Alejandro is next to him…

(Silence).

Agua de Dios was declared a municipality on March 23, 1963.

It is also called the City of Hope.

Maestro Luis Antonio Calvo died on April 22, 1945 at 3:00 p.m.

His last words were:

"The end, an end that never ends. . ."

Acknowledgements

I would like to thank all the people at Agua de Dios who helped me with this book and with the research. To Patricia Devia for always helping when I needed it. To José Israel Castañeda and Efraín Oyaga. To Jhon Jairo Sanchez for his attention and reception at the house of Maestro Calvo.

A special thanks to: Abel Fernando Martínez, MD; Hugo Armando Sotomayor, MD; Director of the Leprosy Museum, María Teresa Rincón; musicologist and composer Susan Campos-Fonseca; musicologist and pianist Luis Gabriel Mesa; musicologist Sergio Ospina and writer and editor Steven P. Miller for his comments, revisions, and teaching.

To the people who pushed me to finish the book: Jorge López, Leonor Garzón, Fernando Vallejo, Diana Camacho, Cristina Palacio, Ramiro Meneses, and Jorge Franco.

To my old friend, Andrés Arias and to my great friend Eduardo Sáenz, for taking me to Agua de Dios for the first time in 2000. For the friendships that bring us together.

To the people in LA where I finished the book in 2007 and that welcomed me into their homes.

To my dear mother-in-law Isabel, who supported me.

To my family, for their love, patience and support: Miguel, Gabi, and Doroteo del Toboso.

"It is useless to think that we can go back to the beginning of everything, without feeling that we are throwing ourselves into a fatuous and desolate void that devours you in the attempt."

J.

Juliandelachica.com

Instagram: @Juliandelachica
Facebook: @juliandelachica

Irreverencegroupmusic.com

Instagram: @Irreverencegroupmusic
Facebook: @Irreverencegroupmusic

CPSIA information can be obtained
at www.ICGtesting.com
Printed in the USA
LVHW041313240523
747905LV00006B/23/J

9 780578 993775

night, in my room, I decided that the best thing to do was to leave Colombia and return to Madrid. I also decided that I would leave the priesthood and spend my life with Esteban. My parents had left me and my sister a small piece of land in the north. I thought we could go there and live in peace. I decided to face it all and sought out María to tell her my plans. It was then that she told me that she was expecting a child: you. At that moment I realized that my destiny was linked to María and to Agua de Dios, and that the life I had was a divine punishment for disobedience and deceit.

I told María that I would give up the absurd idea of following Esteban in exchange for her keeping quiet about the child's paternity. If the priests found out, they would remove me from the congregation and send me back to Spain. I would never see Esteban again. She agreed. The next day she told the Sisters that she was expecting a child and that its conception had been the result of rape. The explanation was not likely to arouse suspicion. In fact, María herself had gone through such experiences. In Agua de Dios rape had become customary, but no one reported it for fear

Esteban faked burns. Then I confided to Imelda that he seemed to have leprosy. As we planned, the murmur was not long in coming. By the next weekend, the whole town was talking about Esteban's health. It was not a difficult scheme. People thought leprosy was contagious. No one was surprised to hear the news that Esteban, a doctor devoted to his patients, might have been infected. The Salesians threw him out of the monastery and he was immediately sent to one of the shelters. Soon his admission was made official, and Esteban, like the others, lost his civil rights. But none of that mattered because we were still together.

One night we woke up hearing gunshots. A group of inmates was trying to escape to look for food. The subsidy was no longer enough. Such unrest was part of the routine now. There was no water and people started to fight like crazy. That night fifteen people died, including Fernando, a great friend, another of the many who was there without any explanation. Rumors about nuns killing the old patients (in name of God!) in order to make space for new patients arose around the town. The situation began to get serious, and I could no longer keep up with my lies. That same